DISCLAIMER

The information contained in *Mind, Muscle, Moksha* is meant for the reader's use as a guide to developing a good physique. No information herein should be construed as medical advice. The information regarding workouts and nutritional suggestions should not be taken as a substitute for professional medical advice. Not all workouts, techniques and dietary practices in this book are suitable for everyone.

The reader should begin an exercise programme only after getting a clearance from his physician who has done his full health check-up. Physique building, when taken to a professional level, comes with a significant risk of injury and the reader should take due care to ensure that he doesn't do damage to his health.

All recommendations contained in this book are made without guarantee on part of the author and/or publisher who, as a result, disclaim any and all liability in connection to use of this information.

ADVANCE PRAISE

Best of luck. You have my best wishes on the book's success.

—**Dave Palumbo**, International Bodybuilder/coach, educator

Good luck. People want knowledge these days.

—**Fakhri Mubarak**, IFBB pro & record-holding coach

Wonderful. My wishes to you for its success.

—**King Kamali**, IFBB pro & coach

Great job, good luck.

—**John Hansen**, Natural Mr Olympia, author of several books

I'm sure your book will be a success, given your experience with clients. You know what works and how to get results.

—**Philip LeGault**, Bodybuilding's Golden Era competitor

Nice job. Keep going.

—**Dr Michael Dusa,** Author, educator

Passion and tenacity overcome a lot. When a person truly believes in something (as you and I do), we don't have to 'hard sell' anyone. The love of what we are 'selling' comes through, and people will be drawn towards what you have. I was truly blessed with my two books, *Flex Appeal* and *Perfect Parts*. They both made it to the New York Times' best sellers list. I attribute it to LOVING what I was sharing. I wish you success!

—**Rachel McLish,** Ms Olympia, author

I wish you all success.

—**Chetan Pathare,** General Secretary
Indian Body Builders Federation (IBBF)

First of all, I would like to congratulate you for your great effort in writing this wonderful book. I wish I had references such as these when I was growing up and trying to make a name for myself as a competitor. This book, I'm sure, will be extremely helpful to anyone who wishes to build a great body or lose fat and get into shape. This will be a true encyclopedia to bodybuilders and fitness enthusiasts. Wish you all the best.

—**Prasad Kumar,** 15-time Mr India, Indian Legend

I went through the full book. You have touched upon every single thing needed to shape the body in all of your 14 chapters. That you have carried pictures of so many of our Indian champions is commendable. Congrats.

—**Mr Arasu,** Mr India, General Secretary Tamil Nadu Amateur Body Building Association (TABBA)

Congratulations. I'm sure this book will be very helpful to all bodybuilders. My wishes to you for its success.

—**Prakash Narasimhan,** National champion & master coach

We all know what to do when we are gifted. We all know what to do when we are rich. We all know what to do when we have a good support system. But, what we do when we don't have all these to push you defines who we are. That's exactly what amazed me so much about Lakshmi Kumar. Success gives us every reason to celebrate, but failure teaches us a lesson. I have always believed that a person who has failed a hundred times can teach us more than a person who succeeded in his first attempt. We don't need people who merely tell us what to do when it comes to bodybuilding and fitness. We need someone who teaches us what we should not do because this field needs mentors who are more cautious with their methods and do not experiment with their clients. Lakshmi Kumar belongs to the former category and I strongly believe that his book will carry the essence of his wisdom acquired over all these years of experience, unbelievable self-discipline and dedication. Trainers are dime a dozen, but a good coach is hard to find. Lakshmi Kumar is a great coach. That explains what one can expect from his book.

—**PT Suresh,** Mr India & Master Coach

In any field, your love for what you pursue is what makes your work special. You cannot be exceptionally good at something when your heart is not in love with what you are doing. Now when I say Lakshmi Kumar has put his heart and soul into this book, I mean every single word of it. *Mind, Muscle, Moksha* is going to be an eye-opener, in the true sense, to readers. Lakshmi Kumar has always been helpful to bodybuilders and fitness enthusiasts – from newbies to corporate workers to professional bodybuilders. The years of hard work he has put in gathering knowledge have helped him build programs giving results to all persons he trained. A man of faith and love, he has his heart at the right place, which makes him so very good at what he is doing.

My hearty congratulations to you on bringing out this book and my best wishes to you and your family!

—**Manoj Sarangapani,** National champion

MIND MUSCLE MOKSHA

Prasad Kumar

Published by
Renu Kaul Verma
Vitasta Publishing Pvt Ltd
2/15, Ansari Road, Daryaganj
New Delhi-110 002
info@vitastapublishing.com

ISBN 978-93-86473-55-4

First Edition 2019
MRP ₹750

Cover Design by Kannan Sundar
Layout by Somesh Kumar Mishra
Printed by Infinity Advertising Services Pvt. Ltd.

MIND MUSCLE MOKSHA

A step by step guide to building a perfect body that is in complete sync with your inner core

LAKSHMI KUMAR

Vitasta
LET KNOWLEDGE SPREAD

TABLE OF CONTENTS

Breaking the Brickwall

Strength does not come from the physical capacity. It comes from an indomitable will. And where there is the will, there is a way. And having known the way, one has to cross several hurdles which pose great challenges and the key to life is accepting these challenges. Once someone stops doing this, he's dead.

But here is the guy, Lakshmi Kumar, who had been with me at *The Hindu* desk and who never stopped doing anything. He fitted into any role, as a journalist, a cine actor, a body builder, a coach and at times speaking spirituality too. No wonder, he has named his book, *Mind, Muscle, Moksha*. The three Ms are, of course, interrelated. Only when a person synchronises his mind and muscle, liberation becomes possible.

Lakshmi, as I used to call him, had time and again proved to me that only those who had respected their body and mind could ever achieve. I knew his parents whose expectations from him had been sky-high and just because they had set a big goal, he had to punish himself day and night to turn them into a reality. In the process, Lakshmi had to shoulder a heavy burden even at the prime of his youth. I had never seen him enjoying life or socialising with friends. He had been devoting all his time only to fulfil the expectations of his parents. Luckily, he had an understanding life partner in Srimathi, who worked harder than him 24 x 7 to help him scale the height.

I myself had at several occasions pointed to Lakshmi the several brick walls along his path, but he just used to tell me, "TAN (as he used to call me), those walls are there for a purpose. They are not going to stop me. They are only giving me a chance to show how badly I want something and they are there only to stop those people who don't want the thing I want."

I personally drew strength and inspiration from this guy, a gem of a person. Of course, a gem cannot be polished without friction nor a man perfected without trials. Like Hanuman, Lakshmi is expanding his body and mind to cross the ocean and I am sure he will soon bring the mountain of solace for all those who are depending on him for their strength. Happy journey ahead Lakshmi.

T A Narasimhan

Managing Editor, *The Hindu*, & novelist

How I See It

Mind Muscle Moksha is a compilation of information that will serve as an invaluable tool to any person who wants to get a great body.

Mind Muscle Moksha reflects my love for bodybuilding and commitment to inform his readers about the various concepts of the fitness and bodybuilding scene in the country. I don't want to make this book look like an encyclopaedia of exercises, simply because such books are already very popular. And, there are plenty of videos from reputable coaches on YouTube that teach a person how do perform every movement.

I put together *Mind Muscle Moksha* to make it the compilation of training techniques, diet, supplements and contest preparation tips I have gathered over years from reputable sources. This book does not limit itself to the hypothesis of one individual but talks about the techniques tried out by many competitors and coaches with good results.

Mind Muscle Moksha will be of immense help to anyone who wants to slip into a posing trunk and don the tanning cream. This book will be as useful to women as it is for men.

Mind Muscle Moksha, though it speaks a lot about bodybuilding, is not meant only for competitive body builders. It has a lot of information which can be used by any individual to lose body fat, get into good shape and stay healthy.

I have also put together a chapter for the bodybuilding brothers, which will throw open the grey and dark sides of the sport – the sweet lies, fraud, abuse and dangers of the grey area.

I can say for sure that *Mind Muscle Moksha* will have answers to several of your questions, if not all, and be an invaluable training partner.

Welcome aboard.

A WORD OF CAUTION

I want to make a few things very clear before you start reading *Mind Muscle Moksha*. And I also want to tell you certain things upfront.

I was proud to be part of the terrific trio – with Olympia Jai and A. Malayaman – that began the fitness movement and took the concepts and benefits of bodybuilding, weight training and nutrition all over Tamil Nadu since 1998. As the other two are strong proponents of natural bodybuilding, a lot of people assumed that I too was natural. However, I have **never** made claims that I was drug-free.

I have been a competitor and struggled to learn a lot of things using the trial and error method. I have certainly experimented with drugs and allowed my friends to use me as a guinea pig.

I always believed in keeping things honest. I am aware of what is happening in the field and am qualified enough to openly state what I have seen.

Internet era

With the arrival of the Internet, information has been spreading across the globe at lightning speed. I see a lot of impressionable youth taking bits and pieces out of books and instruction manuals written by reputable international trainers and contest-preparation coaches, without following all their instructions on training, nutrition and supplements.

Often, beginners and intermediate bodybuilders pick up some programmes that are too advanced for their level.

All these can be extremely harmful to their health in the long run.

Demand and requirements

I regularly interact with the youth at my gym and at seminars and some follow very intense programmes prescribed by celebrity trainers, but fall short in nutrition. They either eat less of the ideal foods or eat the foods that might not be the best choice for their body. I am amused when such people say that elders at home would never allow them to eat enough protein and carbohydrates or take food supplements!

Be warned, if you try to drive your Mercedes or BMW on kerosene, your engine is sure to get ruined.

Such excuses are unacceptable. You should first get convinced that intense training is a serious physical demand and if your body isn't given the right fuel, it is going to cannibalise lean muscle tissue. This, in turn, will slow down your metabolism and make it difficult to lose fat or get into shape. Besides, your immune system will take a serious beating.

Once you read the instructions given in *Mind Muscle Moksha,* convince your elders that you are doing something good for your body. Doing things in an imperfect manner, especially things related to intense physical training (might or might not be competitive bodybuilding) will do more harm than good.

Don't blindly follow information from the Internet as a person needs years of experience to judge what is right and what is wrong, more specifically what is right for his body.

Misinformation and fake gurus

Also remember this – anybody can write anything on the Internet.

Just because it is on the Net doesn't mean that it is correct. A person who claims to be an authority might not be one and you might end up harming yourself following his advice. There are fake 'gurus' who do not reveal their true identity, yet keep offering suggestions.

No professional will give you free advice

keep this in mind. Consider yourself lucky if you find a good-hearted yet knowledgeable person who is ready to help you free of cost. Unless you are sure about the credentials of the person, don't blindly follow his advice on the Internet.

Also, there are greedy people out there who try to swindle young competitors by charging them huge sums for drugs and cycles. As I always suggest, approach a coach of repute and not just one who has a freaky physique or who markets himself well. Do your homework before entrusting yourself to any guru.

My request

As you have picked up *Mind Muscle Moksha*, I suggest you carefully read and understand all my instructions on training and eating right.

Start with the basics and lay a solid foundation for a period of three or four years, remaining totally drug free. Use the information provided here as and when required. Don't change things on your own or just because some expert on the Internet says something different.

Try the advanced techniques presented in *Mind Muscle Moksha* only when you progress to an advanced level. Experiment with unconventional things only if needed.

Good luck.

CHAPTER 1

BENEFITS OF WEIGHT TRAINING

The importance of weight training and the immense benefits it offers to health have been proved scientifically time and again. Several researchers the world over have accepted that weight training, when performed properly and systematically, offers tremendous benefits.

It would be repetitive to state all benefits here as I am sure most of you would be aware of them. However, I have presented some facts that might be of interest to all. These are things you should know before taking up weight training.

Abdul Salim Ansari

Mahendra Chavan

Karthik

Murali Kumar

G Ekamabaram

Baskaran

Manjit Singh

J Muniappan

Kumarananthan

and proper nutrition, might not need very frequent pounding to maintain the size built over the years.

6. Take supplements such as Glucosamine, Chondroitin Sulfate, extra Vitamin C and plenty of water, under proper guidance.

Workouts improve creativity

Researchers at Middlesex University in England have found that those who worked out before being given a task were able to outshine others who didn't train. Workouts improved more than just their mood.

According to sport psychologist Kate Hays, Ph.D, workouts trigger deeper self-awareness.

Psychologists Hays and Wes Sime, Ph.D, at University of Nebraska, have said that they used workouts to trigger creativity in their clients during therapy sessions. According to Dr. Sime, training frees up the individual so that both thoughts and words flow easier.

Judy Torel, therapist, has said that exercise unlocks deeply buried memories that a person does not easily recollect.

Weight training also regulates output of hormones such as testosterone and growth hormone, and releases endorphins. It keeps the metabolism elevated and improves insulin sensitivity so that the body does not store fat. These help a person to maintain health, lean body mass, feel invigorated and above all, attain a sense of accomplishment.

Women need weight training

Weight training does a lot of good for women too. That a woman who trains with heavy weights will build a manly physique is only a myth. Irrespective of the weight with which a woman trains, she just cannot build big, masculine muscles. The reason is simple – a woman's body doesn't produce sufficient day. Sleeping a little more is definitely not a bad idea. Just see to it that you don't eat a meal and immediately go to sleep. The last meal of the day should be low in carbohydrates and high in protein.

Hard working persons need at least 7 ½ to 8 hours of sound sleep every night. If a person can manage to sleep only for 6 ½ hours or so, he or she can compensate for that deficit by taking a nap during the day.

So, eat right, train right and rest enough to ensure good health and appearance.

CHAPTER 2

LEARNING TO WORKOUT

You should have a fair idea about certain phrases and facts before you start working out.

Warm up

These are some exercises you perform to increase blood circulation and get all your muscles – small and big – ready for a workout. These include movements for smaller muscles such as rotator cuff, which lie beneath the shoulders. Warming up properly keeps injuries at bay. Here I am giving you an example

Abhijit Dhavan

Nagesh Prasad

Sarbo Singh

S Senthil Kumaran

T V Pauly

Rajendran Mani

Suhas Khamkar

Pakash Narasimhan

of a warm up programme. You can perform these exercises without weights and with exercise bands or tubes.

Work on the stationary bike for 5 minutes at moderate intensity. Perform myofascial release using a foam roller. This is known as self-myofascial release (SMR). Take time to work your way up. This should be over in 10 minutes. Then do a couple of sets of core activation movements and a few dynamic movements or drills to stretch stiff muscles such as the hips and ankles. Do not perform static stretching when the muscles are cold. Add a few simple exercises to strengthen the stabilizer muscles such as the rhomboids to set your posture right.

Perform movements such as face pulls, shoulder abduction, internal rotation and external rotation. Your total warm-up shouldn't take more than 15 to 20 minutes maximum.

Stretching

There are several types of stretching – static, active, dynamic, PNF and functional stretching.

Static stretching: This is about holding a muscle in a stretched position for 10 or more seconds. This is done after a workout or in between sets. Overdoing this might lead to a decrease in strength and performance.

Active stretching: This is about holding the stretched position with the opposing muscle group, i.e., you hold on to your thighs in such a manner that it stretches the opposing muscle group, hamstrings. A person cannot hold this for more than 5 to 10 seconds.

Dynamic stretching: This is similar to active stretching, but the difference is you don't hold the stretch but keep moving. This is often considered a good way to warm up and also to improve performance.

PNF stretching: Proprioceptive Neuromuscular Facilitation (PNF) is done with the help of a partner or using a towel. This type is believed to use receptors to improve neuromuscular (related to nerves and muscles) response in the body.

Here is an example: To perform PNF on the hamstrings, stretch until you feel a slight discomfort in the muscle. Then contract the hamstring without moving for 3 to 5 seconds. Relax the hamstrings and slowly deepen the stretch using your quadriceps (which is the opposing muscle). Repeat this 3 or 4 times. This technique is believed to improve range of motion and flexibility in a muscle.

Functional stretching: This is performing a series of movements that incorporate stretching. Functional stretching activates and warms up muscles and tendons, without making them too tired. Stretching can be performed after a thorough warm-up. Never perform static stretching before warm-ups because stretching a cool muscle might lead to injury. Please understand that static stretching and warm-up are not one and the same.

Cool down: Similar to warm-up, you perform some movements after your exercises to gradually unwind yourself. These may be gentle arm rotations, swings, gentle static stretches and a few minutes of work on the stationary bike.

Range of motion: The extent of movement in an exercise is known as Range of Motion (RoM). Full RoM means taking a muscle from a fully stretched position to a contracted position. In almost all exercises, it's recommended that you use the full RoM, unless mentioned otherwise.

Breathing pattern: A lot of trainees often confuse themselves when it comes to proper breathing pattern while performing an exercise. Let's keep it simple. The general rule is you inhale while performing the exercise along with gravity and exhale while working against gravity. Things can be slightly tweaked in a couple of movements. In certain exercises, the breath can be released at the completion of the movement. And there are some exceptional cases too. Take the lat pulldown or barbell curl or barbell row. While performing pulldowns, you will hold your breath while pulling the handle towards the chest (working against gravity); while performing barbell curl, you will hold your breath while you curl the barbell towards the shoulders (working against gravity). Some experts say that you have to exhale while you cross the toughest portion of the exercise.

Consider an exercise like the squat. When you squat down with a loaded barbell across your shoulders, you take in a deep breath. Holding your breath, you rise up. Some experts ask you to exhale as you cross the toughest part of the exercise while some recommend that you exhale only after completing the rep. I follow the second method. In general, I tell all my friends not to bother too much about breathing pattern. You can think about breathing when you perform an exercise like the squat or pulldown. On other exercises, I go by what some big names say – "Don't worry about breathing, it will take care of itself."

When to train: Some persons claim that training in the morning hours is the best. However, some researchers say training in the evening hours is better. My suggestion is this – just train some time, morning or evening, than missing a training session. If you are interested in building more muscle, see to it that you have a small meal of protein and slow releasing carbohydrate 2 hours before you hit the weights. This will ensure that your glycogen reserves (carbohydrates stored in the muscle) are full and you are able to train hard. Do NOT train on an empty stomach, and do NOT train within an hour of eating a large meal. You shouldn't be eating huge meals in the first place.

What to wear: Put on clothes that are reasonably loose and allow you to train comfortably. Do not wear clothes that are too tight. Remember, you are in the gym to train properly, not to show off.

Free weights or machines: An ideal programme will make use of free weights predominantly and machines, judiciously. A free weight exercise will not only work the target muscle but also smaller muscles which act as stabilizers. Working on a machine ensures that you train along one plane. Incorporate free weights and machine exercises in your routine in a planned manner and you are on the right track to building a better physique. As a beginner or until you gain decent amount of muscle, use more of barbells and dumbbells. Limit the use of machines.

Just use the lat pulldown, leg press, leg curl and calf raises machines. Other equipment such as the smith machine, pec-deck machine or fancy ones are for very advanced competitive bodybuilders.

How to choose a gym: Now, this is really tough with so many facilities opening up. My suggestion is that you select a place which has enough treadmills, enough free weights, accessories like exercise tubes, foam rollers and all the basic equipment such as a squat rack, and machines for leg curl, hack squat, leg press, calf raise and benches. It should be well-ventilated or fully air-conditioned and maintained properly. Cleanliness on the floor, rest room and maintenance of equipment are also things to be ensured. It's better to choose a place where the trainers are well-informed, friendly and helpful. Keep away from people who waste time and come to the gym only to exercise their vocal chords.

Home gym or commercial gym: I never advise anybody to set up a home gym. Here are my reasons – initial cost; repair and maintenance; lack of motivation to train hard; lack of a training partner to help you while pushing hard; and lack of a spotter to help you perform high-intensity techniques. It's always better to join a commercial gym and leave all unnecessary worry and expenditure at the door.

Requisites of a home gym: If you happen to be person who prefers a home gym, ensure that it has the following equipment: Go to a reputable manufacturer and pick up a sturdy multi-station home gym, which will have attachments to work all major muscle groups. Besides, you will need barbells, weight plates and a pair of adjustable dumbbells. If you intend setting up a hardcore gym to develop your body to the maximum, you should buy the following equipment:

With these, your personal gym will be ready to rock.

1 FLAT/INCLINE/DECLINE ADJUSTABLE BENCH WITH BARBELL RACK

2 LEG CURL/LEG EXTENSION MACHINE (PLATE-LOADING TYPE)

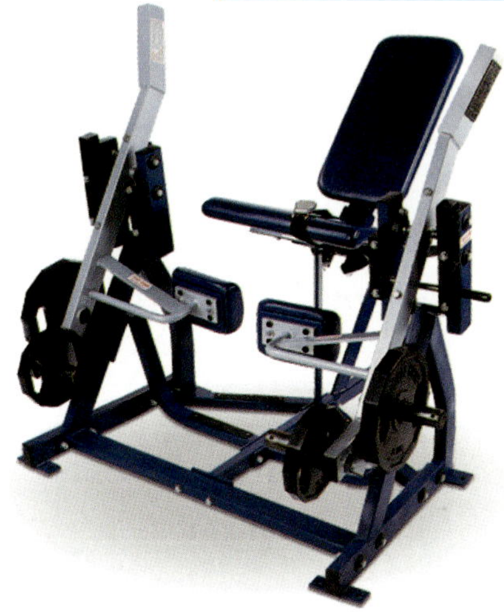

3 PRESSDOWN/LAT PULLDOWN/SEATED ROW MACHINE (PLATE-LOADING OR WEIGHT STACK TYPE)

4 SQUAT RACK

5 BARBELLS

6ft, 5ft, 4ft - 1 each; weight plates – minimum of 150 kg in total (plates can be 1, 2.5, 5, 10, 20 kg); dumbbells – 2 kg, 5 kg, 7.5 kg, 10 kg, 15 kg, 20 kg, 25 kg and 30 kg

Mental aspects: Your mind should be well tuned and prepared before you start on the journey to building a great body. Setting goals before you start a programme is like deciding on a destination before you buy a journey ticket. Your goals should be reasonable and sensible too.

Let's look at an example. If you are fat and have never done any exercise, starting on a programme to build a championship physique or getting a set of ripped abdominals in a few short months is **ridiculous**. Be sensible in choosing your goals. Aim at losing 1 kg of fat every two weeks for the first few months; or aim at gaining 2 to 3 kg of lean muscle in the first 3 months of your systematic training and eating schedule.

Keep short-term goals like adding ¼ inch to the arm in six or eight months of training or losing an inch or two around your waist in six months. Accomplish that, and then set yourself another short-term goal like what you just accomplished. Within a couple of years, your physique will look entirely different from how it looked initially.

Clear visualization

Don't have a hazy picture of what you want to look like after a few years of training. Be very clear as to how you want to look, irrespective of however pathetic you look while you begin. Clear ideas will help you to take clear decisions and help you to stay on track and do whatever it takes to get to your ultimate goal.

But, be reasonable in creating an image too. Do not aspire too much. Here is an example: If you are over 25 and have never been into any sport and are just starting out, do not aspire to win a world championship by the time you are 30 or 32. If you have favourable genes, it **might** happen. But physical recovery might slow down with age and hence, pounding your body in a brutal manner might be too hard on some. This will prevent the body from recovering quickly and growing.

And when you start out, do not always dream of winning the biggest world championship of Mr. Olympia some day. Only 14 men have won it in the past five decades.

According to expert coaches, if you are unable to bench press over 100 kg for

Anand

several reps or squat over 1 ½ times you body weight for 20 reps after three or four years of systematic training and eating, please understand that you do not have the potential to become a world champion. No amount of anabolic drugs or super supplements in the world can change such an ordinary person into a super champion.

However, such a person need not lose hope. Instead, he can set himself short-term goals such as winning a city championship in the next 3 years, a State title in the next 6 years and a medal (Top 3) in the Nationals in 8 to 10 years. That's a pretty good plan, but the person should be extremely dedicated and disciplined to achieve those goals. Depending on the results he gets, he can constantly upgrade his long-term goal.

But always nurture the belief that your goal can be accomplished. If your mind doesn't believe in a particular thing, your body is just not going to cooperate. As long as your goals are reasonable, there is no way you are going to get disappointed. So, believe in yourself and keep working until you succeed.

Vitendar Singh

CHAPTER 3

BUILD MUSCLE AND LOSE FAT

Let me first explain some of the frequently used words in bodybuilding so that you understand things better. Following that, I will give the guidelines on how to begin an exercise programme to build muscle and lose fat. I have briefly mentioned about proper eating and supplements in this chapter. There is an entire chapter devoted to nutrition in this book, which will give more details.

Hira Lal

Premchand Degra

Jai Singh

V Jayaprakash

Mohammed Abdullah

Yatinder Singh

Romy Singh

Bobby Singh

Bhakta Kumar

Ibranta Singh

E G Byju

Beginner

Obviously, he is a person who has just started to train for the first time in his life. A trainee can be referred as a beginner until he completes six months of systematic training and diet plan and has started to display a physique that looks much different from the person who has never been to a gym. A lot of people would have been training mindlessly and eating all the wrong foods, but would have been training for several months. Their physiques will not look like they have worked out at all. These people, though they have been training mindlessly for months, are also classified as beginners.

Intermediates

A person who has put in over six months of systematic training and diet and starts looking bigger and better than those who regularly work out at the gym can be called an intermediate bodybuilder.

Advanced

This is tricky. However, let me put it like this…a person who has trained and eaten the right foods for over two to three years and started looking really impressive alone can be called an advanced bodybuilder.

Ideally speaking, this person should have increased his bodyweight anywhere between 5 and 15 kilogram from his starting weight. He should have gained several inches of muscle on his chest, thighs, shoulders, back, arms and calves. Some persons might not gain a lot of weight, but their muscles would look much bigger and have improved very much in shape. These people alone are considered advanced bodybuilders and not just those who have been frequenting the gym for years without results.

Repetitions (Reps): Moving a barbell, dumbbell or a machine handle from the starting position of an exercise to the finish position one time is known as a repetition or 'rep.'

Sets: A specified number of reps of an exercise performed continuously without rest is known as one set.

Training routine: A complete programme of exercises for each muscle group is known as a routine.

Workout: Often referred to by our Indian bodybuilders as 'practice,' it is just an exercise session done on a particular day.

Carbs: It is the short form of carbohydrates, the macronutrient that provides energy. It used to be known as 'carbo' in the 1980s.

Now, here are some guidelines to begin an exercise programme.

Warm-ups

Always start your workout with a warm-up.

Pyramid principle: This is the most basic technique that can be used by beginners, intermediate trainees and professional bodybuilding champions.

Perform the first set with a light weight (say 12 or 15 repetitions), the second set with a slightly heavier weight (about 10 reps), the third with a little more weight (about 8 reps) and the fourth with the heaviest possible weight (that a particular person can handle in textbook form for about 6 reps).

By gradually increasing the weight set after set, the trainee can thoroughly warm up his muscles before he begins to handle a very heavy weight.

This principle helps to keep injuries at bay.

How many sets?

Do one set of 10 reps on all exercises in the routine throughout the first week. You may perform two sets of 10 reps on all movements the second week (with the same weights). Perform three sets from the third week. From the fourth week, start doing the sets as mentioned in the programme.

From the fourth week, follow the pyramid technique in the exercises mentioned – increase weights on each set while reducing the reps. Workouts can be done 3 or 4 days a week.

Whole-body training & Split system

A rank beginner can start with the three-day routine, training the entire body in a single workout. The next day will be completely for rest, and he will repeat the workout he did the first day on Day 3. The workout will be on 3 non-consecutive days each week. After training like this for the first 3 months, he can use the split system.

The entire body is split and trained in two different workouts in the split system. A trainee works out on Days 1 and 2, takes rest on Day 3, repeats the same workouts on Days

4 and 5, and takes rest on Days 6 and 7.

Three-day routine (Mon, Wed & Fri)

Squats	4 x 15,12,10,8 superset with
Pullovers	4 x 15
Bench press	4 x 15,12,10,8
Bent over rowing	3 x 15,12,10
Military press	3 x 12,10,8
Barbell curl	3 x 12,10,8
Pressdown	3 x 12,10,8
Standing calf raises	3x15,12,10
Crunches	3 x 15

Take complete rest on other days.

Four-day routine (Monday & Thursday)

Squats	4 x 15,12,10,8 superset with
Pullovers	4 x 15
Pulldown	4 x 15,12,10,8
Bent over rowing	3 x 10
Barbell curl	3 x 12,10,8
Incline dumbbell curl	3 x 10
Wrist curl	3 x 15
Standing calf raises	3 x 15,12,10

Wednesday & Saturday

Bench press	4 x 15,12,10,8
Incline dumbbell press	3 x 10

Military press	4 x 15,12,10,8
Lateral raises	3 x 12
Pressdown	3 x 15,12,10
Dumbbell extension	3 x 12
Crunches	3 x 15

Who can use these routines?

Both these routines can be used to build muscle or burn fat. These are the standard and accepted routines that have proved their worth over decades.

These can be used even by advanced bodybuilders to gain more and more muscle. The champs simply have to train harder, heavier, rest more and consume more calories based on their needs. Advanced champions might also change the split as per their requirements.

When to change the workout?

Do not change the workout as long as you keep getting results from the workout you are currently doing. In general, a trainee should do any particular routine for at least 8 to 12 weeks to see maximum results. Changing the routine for the sake of changing is a very bad thing to do. There have been champions who have done the same routine for several months or even years because they continued to get good results.

Rest and recuperation

Exercises lead to small damage in the muscle tissue. This is called micro-trauma. When a person gives enough time between workouts and sleeps well, the damaged muscle fibres recover with the nutrition programme and grow slightly bigger and stronger to face the next training session. Progressively, as the trainee adds more weight and increases the load on the muscles, they keep growing. This is the reason why all muscles should not be worked out every day. Ideally, a muscle group will require 2 to 3 days of rest after a serious workout before it can be trained again. This varies from person to person.

How long to work out?

Do not fix any time duration like you need to train for 1 hour or 2 hours a day. Ideally speaking, a sensible workout session should be over by an hour. If a person keeps training for several hours at a stretch, it means he is not training hard. His muscles would not be feeling every inch of the movement, and obviously, he is not going to see any result. And also remember that if you train really hard, you cannot train long. Training intensity and time duration are inversely proportional. So, avoid marathon workouts and learn the basics well. Keep your workout to the maximum of an hour or else, you might risk overtraining.

Overtraining

When a trainee performs workouts too often or does too many exercises for a muscle or too many sets or too many reps, the damage to the tissue might be excessive. This might initially cause too much pain in the muscle. Over a period of weeks, the body might start eating up the muscle tissue and make the person look bad. Build up of stress will increase and the trainee will experience pain in the entire body and all the joints. He will be extremely irritable, will lose appetite and experience difficulty in sleeping. The immune system will take a serious beating and the person will be prone to infections. A series of health-related problems are sure to follow. These are symptoms of the condition called 'overtraining.' So, it is imperative that a trainee continues to train smart, eat right and takes enough rest.

Experts often compare training, nutrition and rest to the three sides of an equilateral triangle. Unless all the three are perfect, the results will not be up to the mark.

How to start?

If you have never trained with weights and are too lean, start with the first routine given here.

You may do cardio (maximum twice a week, 15 to 20 minutes of walking each session) after you finish weight training. However, if you are very skinny and look literally like a bag of bones, avoid cardio for the first three

months so that you gain some weight and muscle.

If you are chubby, start with the second routine.

Workouts to gain muscle

If you are too skinny and want to gain muscle, do the 3-day routine for 3 to 4 months initially and then do the 4-day split. You may do cardio once or twice a week for 15 minutes after your workout.

If you want to build muscle and are a person who gains weight easily and looks smooth, I would recommend the 4-day workout right away. Perform cardio 3 times a week (20 minutes) at the end of 3 out of your 4 weekly workouts.

When to increase weight?

Anyone who intends to keep gaining muscle has to increase the weights he uses as time progresses.

When do you know that it's time to add weights to the bar or the machine or use the heavier dumbbells?

When you are able to perform about 8 reps in perfect form using a weight with which you struggled to get 6 reps, it is time you increased the weight. Add a little more weight and try to get 6 perfect reps with this new weight. Once you are able to touch 8 again in this new weight, add more weight. This is how you increase the load.

How much weight to add?

Progressively add weights as the weeks go by. The weight

increase should be based on your strength gains. Add in small increments of 1 to 2 kg for smaller muscle groups such as arms, forearms and calves and about 3 to 4 kg for exercises for bigger muscle groups such as legs, back, chest and shoulders. While using dumbbells, you can increase by increments of 1 kg or 1.5 to 2 kg, depending on the availability of dumbbells in your gym.

Workouts to lose fat

Let's assume that you are a person who wants to only lose fat and look fit and trim, and does not want to look like a bodybuilder. Nevertheless, you have to gain at least some lean muscle and maintain it to keep your metabolism high because lean muscle burns more calories even while you are resting. If you don't wish to keep adding more and more muscle, you might not be interested in training heavier and heavier like a bodybuilder as the months go by. So make it a point to always train in the rep range of 12 to 15 for your lower body and 12 reps for your upper body. However, be very meticulous in your weight selection. Choose a weight that will allow you to perform ONLY the set number of reps in textbook form and nothing more. Don't randomly pick a weight and keep doing n-number of reps with it. Rest a maximum of 35 to 40 seconds between sets.

You can do 3-day split or 4-day split, depending on how fat you are. If you have to lose a lot of fat, I would recommend you do the 4-day workout.

You can do your cardiovascular training 4 to 6 times a week

(35 to 45 minutes each session) in the morning. You can drink a cup of black coffee or green tea and then do the cardio. You can hit the weights in the evening.

Diet to build muscle

It has always been suggested to eat 5 to 6 small meals, one meal every 2 ½ to 3 hours. This is believed to build muscle and burn fat.

Consume at least 2.2 gm of complete protein (that provide all amino acids) for every kilogram of your fat-free lean bodyweight. This is generally termed as 1 gm of protein for every pound of lean body weight. Egg whites, grilled chicken breast and fish (Tuna, Indian Salmon, Cod or Seer) are the best sources. Increase calories by consuming more complex carbohydrates that are broken down slowly by the body. Sweet potato, brown rice, fibrous vegetables, whole oats and grains are the best. A person who wants to lose fat and gradually add lean muscle can take anywhere between 1.5 gm to 2 gm of carbs per pound of lean body weight.

To these meals, add a little heart-healthy fats such as macadamia nut oil, evening primrose oil, olive oil (for dressing) and fish oil. Add walnuts and almonds to your diet too. Fruits such as apple, blueberry, guava and one or two small pieces of pineapple or papaya can also be part of your eating plan.

Drink plenty of water, at least 5 to 6 litres a day. Sleep at least for 7 to 8 hours a day. Do not participate in any activity or sport that may burn more calories. Conserve every calorie you consume to build muscle.

Supplements

Take a top quality multi-vitamin/multi-mineral pill with breakfast every day. Go with a reputable brand that makes such supplements keeping athletes in mind and not sedentary persons. A lot of coaches recommend taking 1,000 mg of vitamin C split into 3 or 4 doses along with your meals is good. However, not all researchers agree with this. They contend that you might need this amount of extra vitamin only if your diet is deficient in it. So, it's more a matter of individual's decision.

Adding a good quality whey protein before and after a workout and immediately after waking up will be extremely helpful. More details can be found in the chapter on nutrition and supplements. Essential fats and psyllium husk are invaluable tools. Do not ignore them.

Diet to lose weight

I personally recommend that even a person who does not want to be a bodybuilder but only lose fat should also initially consume at least 2 gm to 2.2 gm of complete protein for every kilogram of fat-free lean bodyweight. His carbs should be between 1 gm to 1.5 gm per pound of fat-free bodyweight. This will help him gain some lean muscle, thereby increasing metabolism.

If the person feels he is gaining a lot of muscle (which, however, will not happen immediately), he can slightly reduce his calories by cutting down protein to 2 gm per pound of lean body weight. Once a desired amount of lean muscle is built, he can calculate his Basal Metabolic Rate (BMR), his daily calorific expenditure and take only that many calories so that his body weight and muscle mass stay at that point and do not increase further. More details on BMR can be found in the chapter on nutrition and supplements.

As far as general diet recommendations are concerned, avoid all junk food, sugar, fruit juices, syrups and bottled drinks. Eat green vegetable salads instead of rice or juices. Drink plenty of water. Use essential fats in the right amount or else you will not lose enough body fat. Sleep at least for 8 hours. Supplements can be taken like mentioned earlier.

New studies

Even as I was writing this book, I happened to interact with an extremely successful world class coach, who asserted that frequent meals have no direct link with increased metabolism. He recommended only 2 gm of protein per kilogram of lean body weight. He also said that only a huge pro bodybuilder weighing a ripped 250 or 300 pounds might need 5 or 6 small meals a day, more so because he just cannot get enough protein, carbs and fat by eating 3 meals. Others can still get all the protein and carbs in three meals and need not necessarily force themselves into eating 5 or 6 times a day.

These recommendations are presented here not to confuse you. The very idea of this book is to present various training techniques and suggestions so that you try them out and see what suits you the best. There is nothing wrong in trying to eat just three meals a day like mentioned here. Try it out. If you feel your body is not responding much to it, follow the conventional path.

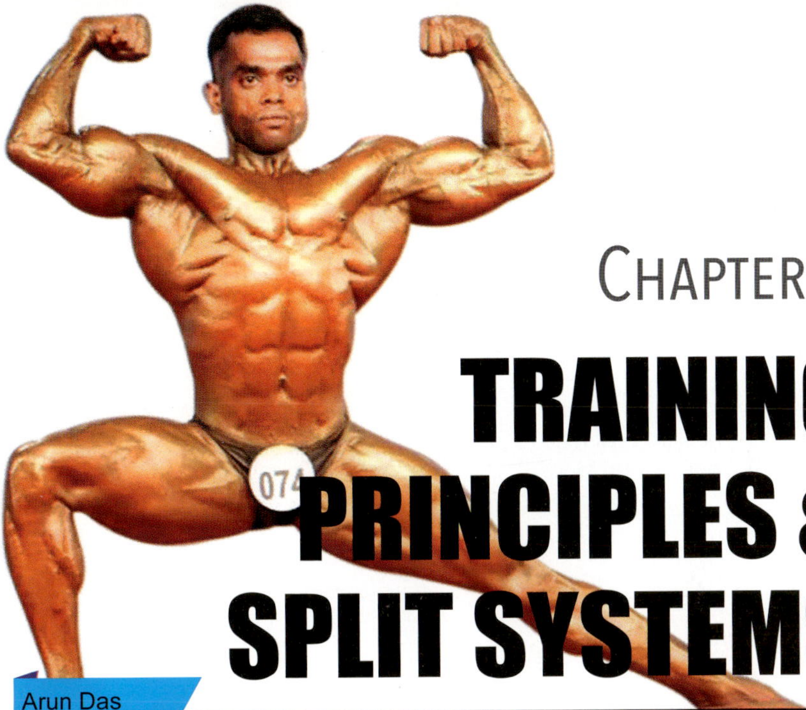

Arun Das

CHAPTER 4

TRAINING PRINCIPLES & SPLIT SYSTEMS

There are several training principles or techniques that help in building muscle. And there are several types of split systems too. I have explained some of the best and most-productive techniques and training splits in this chapter. However, some of the advanced principles explained here are not for a beginner or an intermediate bodybuilder. Only those who have been training hard and eating right for at least a year and gained significant amount of muscle mass can try out many of these techniques. At least for one year, train

Y Annamalai

M Kothandaraman

Kamaraj

Mohan Subramaniam

Karanjit Singh

Mansoor Basha

Bihari Lal
Anas Husain
Arunachalam
Kandan
K L N V Prasad
Ashok Das
Ankur Sharma
Sunil Aptekar
hundrakpam
radipkumar

anveer Akram

Shiv Kumar
90
life eakness is

Parvesh
Kumar

V C Rojas

ee John

Ambar Sharma

Shyam Sundar

Sunit Jadhav

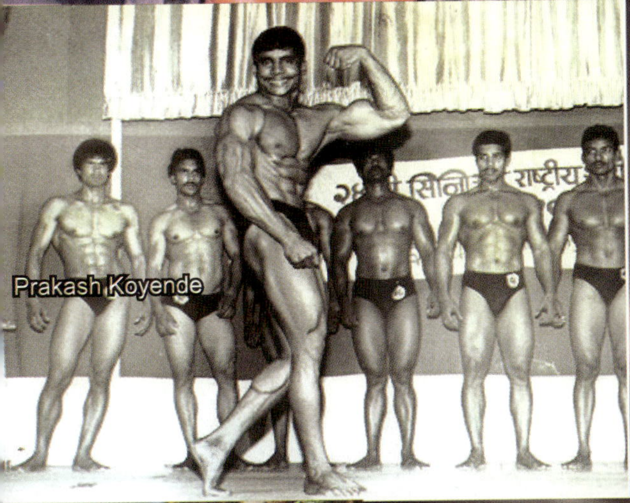
Prakash Koyende

Nitin Mhatre

Ram Nivas

Vimal Anand

Sagar Katurde

Javed Ali Khan

P T Suresh

Amit Chaudhary

Arumugam

N Mohanarangam

Manoj Majumdar

Anoop Raju

A P Joshy

S K Mustaque

Ashish Sakharkar

V M Basheer

using the basic split using basic exercises and gain maximum amount of muscle. After a year's serious training and after laying a solid foundation, start using some of these techniques judiciously so that you shock the muscles into growth without overtraining.

Training smart, as I have said so many times, is what will help once you have crossed the beginner and intermediate stage in bodybuilding. Advanced bodybuilders who have been into serious training for more than two years can try all the techniques in a planned manner and find out what all work well for them.

Double split system

I had explained in Chapter 3 about the split system.

A double-split system is one in which a trainee works out twice a day. He will train a couple of muscles in the morning, have a few meals once in 2 ½ or 3 hours, and come back for a second workout later in the evening and train a different muscle group. For example, you can train chest and shoulders in the morning, and come back for triceps and abs in the evening. Training more than one or two muscles in a single workout can be too taxing. By splitting the workout into two, you can prevent that from happening. This system will be greatly helpful during competition preparation because the trainee might not have the strength and energy he had in the offseason. This technique burns lot of calories too, which is beneficial while trying to burn fat for a contest.

A person who can and wants to train only four days a week using this system can train as follows:

Mon and Thu: Chest and shoulders in the morning; triceps and abs in the evening

Tue and Fri: Back and biceps in the morning; legs in the evening

Wed, Sat, Sun: Rest A person who is soft and wants to train 6 days a week using this system to elicit maximum fat loss can do it as follows:

Mon and Thu: Chest and shoulders in the morning; triceps and abs in the evening

Tue and Fri: Back and calves in the morning; biceps and forearms in the evening

Wed and Sat: Thighs in the morning; hamstrings and gluteus in the evening

Triple split system

In this system, a trainee works out three times a day! This can be done only by a very few people who have abundance of time for training and eating every day. However, I do know certain persons who have somehow squeezed out three workouts despite not having an entire day at their disposal.

Ideally speaking, a triple-split workout routine should be short and get over within 30 minutes. Here is an example: you can train your chest using 3 or 4 exercises in the morning, have a couple of small meals, then train the shoulders later in the afternoon, have a couple of small meals and finally train the triceps at night. End the day with another small meal after the third workout. By training more than once a day using short yet intense workouts, the body will release more natural growth hormone. This will help the trainee to get leaner. The body will constantly keep burning calories and help the person gain muscularity fast. This will be very helpful while getting ready for a contest because anyone who diets hard will find it difficult to train 2 or 3 muscles in the same workout. Such persons will immensely benefit from this split. However, doing too many exercises or lengthy workouts three times a day will lead to overtraining and ruin the physique. Be smart if you want to try this split.

Super set training principle

Performing one set of an exercise for a particular muscle and quickly doing a set of another exercise for the muscle found opposite is known as super-set training. After a minute's rest, the superset can be repeated for two or three more times in the same manner with one minute rest in between.

For example, you can train biceps and triceps; chest and back; thighs and hamstrings; and front and rear head of the shoulders using this technique.

This technique gives a tremendous pump, flushes more blood into a particular region and facilitates growth when performed in the offseason. When performed during contest preparation, this technique burns lot of calories and helps a trainee get a lean look faster.

While trying out this principle, do not perform more than four exercises for the bigger muscles such as thighs, chest and back. Do not perform more than three supersets for smaller muscles such as arms and shoulders.

Compound sets training

This is a technique in which you perform two exercises for the same muscle without taking rest. For example, you can perform a set of incline dumbbell curl and immediately a set of preacher curl. After a minute's rest, the compound set can be repeated two more times in the same manner with one minute's rest between the combos. This is a technique used by advanced bodybuilders to shock a particular muscle into more growth.

Tri-sets training

Here, you perform three different exercises for the same muscle group without taking rest between the sets. Do not perform more than three trisets for smaller muscles such as arms and not more than four trisets for bigger muscles such as chest, legs and back.

Giant sets training

Performing four or five different exercises for the same muscle group without rest between the sets is known as a giant set. A trainee should not do more than 3 giant sets for any muscle group because that itself would come to 15 total sets (at least). Anything more might lead to overtraining and muscle loss. This technique can be judiciously used to shock a muscle group. It's better not to do this technique for more than five or six weeks.

Do not perform giant sets for all muscles at the same time. Select just one or two muscles and train them using this principle.

Combination sets principle

Performing a set of bench press for the chest and without rest doing a set of chinning for the back is called a super set. When you do a set of bench press, then rest for about 1 minute and then do a set of chinning, it is called a combination set. This is believed to work very well in gaining muscle. Former Mr. Olympia Sergio Oliva reportedly used this technique and got great results.

Pre-exhaust principle

This is a technique that helps to shock stubborn muscles and leads to growth. You will be doing two exercises in super set fashion in this technique for a particular muscle. The first exercise will be a single-joint exercise, also called isolation exercise. The second exercise is a compound movement, also known as multi-joint exercise. When you do an isolation exercise like dumbbell flye for the chest, the shoulders do not get worked. You pre-exhaust only the chest and then when you immediately superset it with bench press, the chest, which is already working, will get more stimulation than the shoulders. This will help the persons who always say that they don't feel much in their chest while doing bench press. This technique can be used almost on all muscles.

It can be performed in the off-season too, but it is very helpful while preparing for contests.

Post-exhaust technique

This is the reverse of the pre-exhaust technique. Here, you do a set of compound exercise and quickly follow it up with an isolation exercise. This is also to shock stubborn muscles into growth. This technique, too, helps a lot during contest training.

Progressive overload principle

This is a principle I learnt from one of respected masters in Tamil Nadu. This can be effectively used by an intermediate bodybuilder to gain muscle.

Generally, to gain more muscle in the shortest possible time, a whole body routine is recommended. A trainee will be asked to do only the basic exercises, 3 non-consecutive days a week like Monday, Wednesday and Friday. The routine will have squats, bench press, barbell row, barbell shoulder press, barbell curl, barbell extension and calf raises.

After a whole-body warm up, start the first exercise. All exercises should be done for 4 sets using the same weight. Load the barbell with a weight which is 50% of your 1 rep maximum (1RM) and do a set. Do not count the reps. Keep doing the reps until you reach a point where you are unable to do any more strict rep without stopping for a while. This is called

In this technique, you do only ONE exercise for a muscle group. Let us assume that you are going to do leg press for the thighs.

After one or two warm up sets, load the leg press machine with a light weight (but certainly not a weight that will allow you to do get even 100 reps) and do 50 reps. It need not be non-stop 50 reps. You can do 30 reps non-stop, then pause for a second or two and then do 4 or 5 more, then pause again for a few more seconds and then do 4 or 5 reps again. In this manner complete 50 reps. Take a break of 40 seconds to maximum 45 seconds. Slightly increase the weight and now do 40 reps in the manner mentioned before. As said earlier, weight selection should be meticulous. Then after 40 to 45 seconds rest, increase the weight and do 30 reps. Then rest for 45 seconds, increase the weight and do 20. The rest again, increase weight and do 10 reps.

This weight will be the weight which will allow you to do exactly 10 reps. You can choose the weights in all the earlier sets keeping this weight in mind.

Do 10 reps, rest for 45 seconds. Then do another set of 10 reps with the same weight.

After 45 seconds rest, reduce the weight and do a set of 20 reps. Rest, reduce the weight and do a set of 30 reps. Rest again, reduce the weight again and do a set of 40 reps. Then rest again, reduce the weight again and do the last set of 50 reps. That's it. Just 1 exercise and your thigh workout is over.

This technique has helped a lot of champions in building

muscle while getting that lean, quality look. It's generally done in the off-season, but I have seen some competitors doing it even in their contest prep.

Fascia Stretch Training (FST-7)

This is a training routine created and promoted by Hany Ramrod, who has trained some of the greatest champions like Phil Heath.

This technique has been used by champions for all their muscles or any one or two muscles which they feel need special attention.

"F" of the FST signifies fascia which surrounds the muscles. It is a belief that the fascia layer should be stretched for the muscles to get bigger. That brings us to the "S" of FST, which stands for stretch. The usual stretching performed between sets or after exercise have their place. However, getting a great stretch in the fascia because of a huge pump even while exercising is believed to facilitate growth. That brings us to the last word or number in the name,

Arun Shokeen

"7." This stands for the number of sets one has to do using this technique. This FST-7 technique is generally used on the last exercise done for a body part in which a trainee does 7 sets of 12 reps with only 30 seconds rest between them. This FST technique is generally done on an isolation movement, though some advanced bodybuilders do even exercises like leg press or hack squats using this.

I will explain with an example. First, do 2 or 3 compound exercises for the chosen muscle and have an isolation movement as the last exercise. Do 7 sets of 12 reps with 30 seconds rest between them.

Pre-load and over-load

This is an advanced variation of FST-7. For the pre-load part, you begin the first exercise with FST-7 technique. You then go on to do 2 exercises using normal technique and for the overload part, you finish the muscle with the final exercise using FST-7 technique. So, you might be doing 3 to 4 different exercises for a particular muscle with FST-7 technique on the first and last exercises. However, this variation might be tremendously hard on your recovery and even the joints, especially when you train legs. So, care should be taken so that you train smart based on your recovery.

The FST-7 technique is generally done in off-season with great results. Nevertheless, there are champions who do it even while getting ready for a contest.

Priority training principle

This is a very simple technique. Let us assume that your calf muscles are weak and you generally train it with your back. On the workout day, do not start with your back exercises. Instead, start with exercises for your calves. This will ensure that you hit those muscles when you are fresh and are able to stimulate maximum response. This is prioritising your weak muscles so that you can work them very hard.

However, if your triceps are weak and you generally train chest, shoulders and triceps together, do not start with your triceps. If you do so and your triceps are fatigued, you will not be able to push hard on chest and shoulders. In such cases, try doing arms workout on a separate day and prioritise your triceps or try other techniques for your triceps so that you hit them hard for maximum development. Think well and use these techniques.

Supplementary training principle

This is a very unconventional technique and not found in training manuals. Some competitors have found doing this beneficial and hence made it a practice.

If your rear deltoids are weak, do 3 or 4 sets of an isolation exercise for that head every day at the beginning of your workout. Do them fast with minimum rest between sets. Go for a full range of motion and squeeze the muscle well at the top.

You can either do the same exercise every day or a different exercise. This technique, however, should not be done throughout the year. It's generally done in the last 6 weeks of a contest preparation. As explained in the previous technique, this kind of training should not be done on all muscles as well because it might affect the training intensity on the exercises that follow. This is generally restricted to exercises for rear delts and movements done to enhance muscularity in the back.

Circuit training

This is a principle that will help a person burn fat and get leaner while improving cardiovascular endurance. Here is how it is done. Warm up all your muscles and joints well. Choose 5 exercises for the upper body and 5 for the lower body. Do 1 set of 10 to 12 reps on the first upper body exercise and without resting, do 1 set of 10 to 12 reps on the first lower body exercise. Without resting, do 1 set of 10 to 12 reps on the second exercise chosen for the upper body and immediately do 1 set of 10 to 12 reps on the second exercise selected for the lower body. In this manner, do 1 upper body movement and without resting do 1 lower body movement until you have done 1 set on all the exercises chosen. You have now completed 1 circuit. Take a break for two minutes by gently walking around. Then do a second circuit and then rest for two minutes. In this manner, totally perform 4 to 5 circuits. This workout is done twice a week with two days rest between training days or thrice a week on non-consecutive days.

Cardio can be performed 2 to 4 times a week on non-workout days or separately in the mornings, depending on the individual's recuperative ability and requirements.

Selection of weight should be meticulous to ensure best results. Doing 12 reps with a weight with which you can actually do 25 reps to failure is not going to yield great results. Your reps should come extremely close to failure.

1 ½ reps principle

Let us assume that you are going to do barbell curls as your first exercise for biceps. Using this technique, you will first be doing a half rep – lift the barbell from the bottom position until it is parallel to the ground and then lower it to the start position. Then do a full repetition. Repeat this. This technique will give a great pump and can be used either to shock growth out of a stubborn muscle or during a contest prep. You have to make changes in the total training volume (number of sets and reps) and diet and cardio, depending on whether you use this technique in off-season or during contest preparation.

Muscle confusion principle

If a person keeps training using the same exercises, sets, reps and technique, his body is likely to get adapted to the training stimuli and might stop responding. This is why we recommend that a trainee change the split or sets and reps or exercises once in 3 or 4 months or when the body stops making progress in appearance, strength or power. Advanced bodybuilders who have been training for years might very quickly get adapted to any programme and their bodies might stop responding even a few weeks or days after they start a new programme. So, such advanced guys can do changes in every workout and this keeps the body guessing as what might come next. This is known as muscle confusion principle.

The changes can be as simple as changing the order of exercises. A person can do new exercises or try new techniques every workout.

Instinctive training principle

This is closely connected to the previous technique. Consider this example. Some very advanced bodybuilders won't have a training routine at all. They might just go to the gym and train whatever muscle they feel like training that day. However, they will ensure that they train all muscles equally hard and that there are no weaknesses. This is known as instinctive training. This should be done only by very advanced champions like top pros. I have explained this principle for information purpose. Please do not lose control and start doing things that are beyond your level.

Staggered sets principle

Let me explain this technique with an example again.

Assume that your calves are weak. You will need very hard training on a regular basis to make them respond. If you relegate calf exercises to the end of your workout after training a major muscle like chest or back, you might not be fresh enough to pound the calves hard. So, after a set of bench presses or chinning, quickly do a set of standing calf raises instead of resting for a full minute. After a gap of 10 to 15 seconds or a little more, do the second set for the bigger muscle and immediately after that, do a second set of calf raises. In this manner, you can do calf training even as you pound the upper body. This is called staggered sets training.

Joe Weider says that you can do one set of chest, then do one set for thighs and then one set for the calves. You may then rest for a short while and repeat the exercises in the same order until you complete the number of sets you want to do. Weider says this principle is based on the fact that the larger muscle groups recover while you train the smaller muscle groups.

Drop sets or descending sets or stripping method

This is a technique in which you do a set till you are unable to do any more reps. Let us assume that you did 10 reps and could not do more. This is called training to failure. Once you reach failure, reduce the weight by 20 to 30 % and try to do another set of 10 reps. The weight reduction should be in such manner that you are able to get 10 reps even on this set. Once you reach failure on the 10th rep, drop the weight again and get 10 more reps.

This is called drop set technique. It is also called stripping technique when it is done with a barbell where you keep removing weight plates after each set.

Doing too much of this might result in overtraining. So, this is a technique for advanced bodybuilders who can clearly realize how much their body needs and when to stop.

Running the rack & Up-and-down the rack

Let us train shoulders using these techniques. After a thorough warm up, choose a pair of dumbbells heavy enough that will allow you do perform exactly 6 reps. Do those 6 reps, and immediately after completing the set, grab a pair of dumbbells weighing 5 lbs less and do another set of 6 reps. Keep going down until you reach the lightest weight. This is running the rack technique.

As regards 'Up-and-down-the rack' technique, grab a light pair of dumbbells and do a set presses for 6 reps. Put down the weight, take the next heavier pair and do another set of 6 reps. Keep going up the dumbbell rack handling the bigger weights. Once you do the heaviest weight for 6 reps, take the second heaviest weight and do 6 reps. Reverse the process until you come back to the lightest weight. Both these techniques are prone to be abused. So use them judiciously.

Forced-reps training principle

Doing a couple of reps with some help from your training partner after you reach failure on an exercise is called forced reps principle. Such forced reps should not be done on every set of every single exercise. There are experts who say that this should be done on the last set of an exercise alone. It might lead to overtraining if done on every single exercise. However, advanced bodybuilders can use it sensibly to increase training intensity and trigger more growth.

Just don't start so heavy that your partner is compelled to help you from the very first rep.

Rest-pause principle

Let us assume that you are doing leg press and you hit failure on the 10th rep. You might still be able to do a couple of more reps with the same weight. So, on reaching failure at 10, stop the set for say 10 seconds and then do another set till failure. Once you reach failure again, rest and then do another set. This is rest-pause technique and it helps to build muscle.

This technique can be used well to gain lot of strength as well.

After a good warm-up, start your set with a weight that will allow you to perform exactly 3 reps or 5 reps (3 rep maximum or 5 rep maximum). After finishing 3 reps, rack the weight, rest for 15 seconds and then do another rep. Repeat this process until you finish 4 to 6 reps in this manner. This concludes one rest-pause set. This technique is very effective for making gains in strength.

Burns & Partial reps

This is a technique in which you keep training beyond failure. On reaching failure on an exercise like barbell curls, you can lift the weight just for a few inches and lower it again. This kind of half reps increase lactic acid build-up in the muscle and make you feel as if the biceps are on fire. Hence the name burns or partial reps. Try this technique only on select exercises like those for biceps and delts. It will be sensible if you do not try this on exercises like squats.

Quality training principle

Here you gradually reduce the rest between sets while still maintaining or increasing the number of reps performed. Let us say you want to do 4 sets of 10 reps on the barbell curl. After the first set of 10, rest for 30 seconds and do the second set of 10. Rest only for 20 seconds and do the second set of 10. Then rest for 15 seconds and do the third set of 10. Rest for 10 seconds and do the last set of 10. This is believed to be very helpful in contest prep as it increases oxygen demand and also increases GH spurt.

Cheating training principle

This is a technique under which you can slightly and in a controlled manner swing a heavy weight so that it crosses a sticking point and allows you to handle a poundage which you otherwise would not have been able to handle.

Here is an example. Load the barbell with a weight which is heavier than what you use for 8 reps. Slightly bend your knees, get a thrust upwards from the thighs and it will help you lift the barbell from the hanging position and complete the curl. However, while lowering the weight, it should come under full control and you have to fight it hard to keep the descent perfect. This is a cheat rep and this technique should be used only on exercises like the barbell curl and shoulder presses. It would be sensible that you avoid it on squats, rows and deadlifts.

Power cleans, clean and jerk, snatch and high pulls are exercises in which this principle is applied. By using this sensibly, you can build a lot of strength and power.

Negatives or eccentric training

This is a technique that helps to gain a lot of strength. Let us take an example of bench press and analyse this principle. After warming up well, load the barbell with a weight that is 105% of your one rep maximum (1 RM). Lift the barbell off the rack with a partner's help. Slowly lower it with no help from your partner taking about 3 to 4 seconds. The lowering should be slower than it is while doing a regular set. Once you reach the bottom position, press it up with your partner's help. Lower it again slowly using your own strength and press it up again with help. Do this again for a third rep and take a few minutes rest. Do 2 more such sets of only negative reps and your chest workout is over. If you do anything more, it will lead to overtraining and short-circuit your gains. If you are able to do more than 6 reps as pure negatives, it means the weight selected has to be increased.

This training is adopted purely for strength building. With more strength, you will slowly be able to handle more weight on the regular sets, which will help you gain muscle size too.

Double pyramid and reverse pyramid training principles

A double pyramid is one in which you first do 4 sets of say 15,12,10 and 8 reps as you do in the regular pyramid technique. Once you finish the last set, take a minute's rest and reverse what you have done. Do 10,12, and 15 reps decreasing the weight while taking short rest between sets. This technique trains all kinds of muscle fibres.

In the reverse pyramid, warm up well using 2 or 3 light sets. Then load the barbell with a heavy weight that will allow you to perform only 5 to 6 reps to failure and get those reps. After 1 ½ minutes rest, slightly reduce the weight and do 8 reps. After a minute's rest, reduce the weight further and do 10 reps. After 45 to 60 seconds rest, reduce more weight and do 12 reps. After 30 to 40 seconds rest, drop more weight and do 15 reps. This is the reverse pyramid principle.

Both these techniques build strength and size. However, the double pyramid is slightly more effective in building size.

I-go you-go principle

As the very name suggests, this is a principle which states that you do a set of say 10 reps and quickly hand over the barbell to your partner for him to do 10 reps. As soon as he finishes it, he returns the barbell to you and you do your second set of 10 reps. Then you give the barbell to him for his second set.

This builds competitiveness, sportsmanship and camaraderie among champions and keeps rest to a minimum. This was used by yesteryear champions while getting ready for contests.

Cumulative reps principle

In this technique, you load the barbell with a weight you can do 10 prefect reps on say the bench press. With this weight do only 1 rep and rest for 10 seconds. Then do 2 reps with the same weight and rest for 10 seconds. Now do three reps with this weight, rest for 10 seconds and do 4 reps. Keep going up and try to get 10 reps finally. You might not be able to get more than 7 or 8 reps. It is fine. The pump you get from this technique will be awesome and this is a great technique to shock the muscles into growth. It has been used by some champions even in contest training.

21s training or Platoon system

I will explain using the barbell curls as an example. Load the barbell with 50% of the heaviest weight you can do. From the bottom position, do the bottom 1/3 rep, i.e., raise the barbell until it reaches a point in which the forearms are parallel to the ground and lower it. Do 7 such 1/3 reps. Then hold the bar at a level in which your forearms are parallel to the ground. This will be the midpoint of the usual barbell curl. From this point, curl the weight up to the top position. This is the top 1/3 rep. Lower the bar to the midpoint position. Do 7 such reps. Then do 7 full range reps. You would have done 21 total reps.

This is a technique which can be used even in shoulder, chest and triceps training. However, use it for contest prep on the last exercise for a muscle and not as a primary mass building technique.

Peak contraction training principle

Jagdish Lad

This is a principle which says that at the top position of any rep, hold the squeeze for 3 seconds and lower the weight. This is believed to bring a more lean and quality look to the muscle group. However, some modern-day experts say that a fully contracted position is not the position where the muscle is fully shortened (end of the movement.) They say that maximum contraction is somewhere in the middle.

I personally feel that mid-points are perfect for isometric work on exercises like lateral raises. So, if you decide to try this, see which positions allow maximum contraction and then do them. Posing and squeezing the muscles between sets will be of tremendous help to bring muscle hardness and quality as well.

Iso-tension principle

This is simply another name for flexing. After you finish a set of triceps pressdowns or close-grip bench press, extend you arms fully and flex your triceps hard for 6 to 10 seconds. You can try this on all muscle groups. This is a technique practiced religiously in contest preparation. Doing it in off-season will be of immense help to you as well.

Y3T or Yoda Three Training

This training system was developed by bodybuilder/coach Neil Hill. Here, a person trains with various rep ranges each week for 3 weeks. This pattern is repeated two more times, making it a 9-week training programme.

During week 1, choose two or three basic exercises (compound movements) for each muscle. After a couple of warm up sets, do 3 sets of 6 to 10 reps on each exercise. This is a heavy-weight workout week.

During week 2, do the two or three basic exercises like the previous week. However, reduce the weight slightly and perform 10 to 14 reps on each set. Along with these two or three compound movements, add an isolation exercise and do 3 sets of 10 to 14 reps on that too. This is a moderate-weight workout week.

exercises such as bicep curls and triceps extensions, the temp should be 3-0-2.

Choose exercises that recruit a lot of muscle mass for the big muscles such as squats and bench presses.

Don't train a muscle group more than once in every four or five days as you will need a lot of time for complete recovery.

Increase weight

When you are able to do 10 sets of 10 with a constant rest interval between sets, increase the weight by 5%.

Do not use intense techniques such as forced reps, negatives or burns.

Intermediate training Phase 1

After you train using GVT for 6 workouts, you can increase the demand by doing 2 exercises for each muscle. However, on the first basic exercise for a given muscle, do 10 sets of 10 reps as usual with a tempo of 4-0-2. Take 90 seconds between sets. After this, do a basic exercise for the other muscle in this manner.

After doing 10 sets of 10 on one basic exercise for the two muscles, choose another exercise for the first muscle and do 3 sets of 10 to 12 reps 3-0-2 temp. Take only 60 seconds rest between sets.

After this, do an exercise for the second muscle 3 sets of 10 to 12 reps using the 3-0-2 temp resting only 60 seconds.

Here is an example of chest and back day.

*Incline dumbbell press 10 sets of 10 reps with a tempo 4-0-2 and rest of 90 seconds between sets.

*Reverse grip 10 sets of 10 reps with a tempo 4-0-2 and rest of 90 seconds between sets.

*Decline dumbbell flyes 3 sets of 10-12 reps with a tempo of 3-0-2 taking 60 seconds rest between sets.

*One-arm dumbbell row 3 sets of 10-12 reps with a tempo of 3-0-2 taking 60 seconds rest between sets.

Intermediate training Phase 2

After doing six workouts of the 5-day cycle as mentioned earlier, begin a 3-week cycle. Here, you will be doing 6 to 8 reps and only 4 to 6 sets per body part. After 3 weeks of this training, go back to the original GVT, but do 10 sets of 6 reps. On exercises where you have to do 10 sets, use a weight which will allow you to do 12 reps but do only 6 reps.

Advanced trainee programme

Experts recommend using the technique of 5% method. That is, the trainee should increase the weight by 4 to 5% every workout for two workouts in a row. He should then reduce the rep target by one rep for every weight increase. The weight will then be reduced by 5% once again and the reps increased to the original starting point.

Here is an example.

Let us say you can do barbell curls with 100 pounds for 12 strict reps. If you are unable to increase the reps or weight on

PHA training

This stands for Peripheral Heart Action. This is similar to circuit training. However, there is a difference. In circuit training, you will be doing a series of 10 to 12 exrecises non-stop, alternating between one upper body exercise and one lower body exercise. In PHA, you will do 5 or 6 exercises non-stop alternating one upper body movement and one lower body movement. After resting for 1 minute, you can repeat the sequence again. Do 3 to 5 such rounds. As you progress, reduce rest periods to a minimum between rounds. When you are aerobically more conditioned, you can do a second series of different exercises for 3 to 4 rounds.

Here is an example:

1 sequence (for those who start for the first time)

Incline dumbbell press	6 reps
Squat	8 reps
Barbell over rows	6 reps
Stiff-legged deadlift	8 reps
Hanging knee raise	8 reps

PHA helps big time in fat loss and improving muscular endurance. For fat loss, train on three non-consecutive days a week and keep adding intensity by doing more than one sequence for 4 to 5 rounds each as you progress.

Do not perform cardio on the other days as it might lead to overtraining.

There are some experts who say that PHA can be used even in a strength building programme. If you want to try that, train using the five sets of five reps for two days a week, say Monday and Thursday. Choose 4 or 5 basic exercises for major muscle groups and do them for 5 sets of 5 reps each. On two other days, like Wednesday and Saturday, do moderate PHA with just one sequence and five rounds on that.

Now, with all those training techniques explained, let me explain some training systems, how to determine your muscle fibre type and also how to make certain training routines.

High octane cardio (HOC) training

This is a training system that burns fat at an incredible rate. The only problem is that it cannot be done by extremely overweight individuals, the aged or persons with joint problems.

Known as high octane cardio (HOC), this type of training, I believe, is used by boxers. They call it 'Roadwork.'

How boxers do it

Jog fifty yards and immediately and do a set of push ups and crunches, 25 reps on each exercise. Get up immediately and start jogging again for another 50 yards.

Repeat the push ups and crunches sequence. Continue this cycle for several minutes. This kind of training builds up cardiovascular and muscular endurance. It burns a lot of calories obviously.

Alternatives

You can also combine cardio training such as jogging and rope jump (skipping) with certain ballistic weight training exercises such as dumbbell swing, dumbbell snatch and dumbbell clean and jerk. These exercises work several large muscle groups at the same time and burn a lot of calories. You will also use the entire body as one unit, which might increase coordination. Combat athletes will develop speed and power from ballistic exercises.

Beginner training

Place a dumbbell on a track field and another dumbbell on the opposite side of the field. Start jogging. When you come to one of the dumbbells, pick it up and do 20 reps of dumbbell swing. Put the weight down, jog to the other dumbbell and do 20 reps of dumbbell clean and jerk.

This is called one lap. Perform four such laps.

The workout may take about 10-15 minutes depending on how fast you jog and how fast you train.

Eventually do eight laps.

Advanced training

Place four dumbbells on the field at four different points. Perform the training as before, jogging from one dumbbell to another.

So, one lap will now have four sets of exercise and four small bouts of jogging.

Eventually perform four laps and then work up to eight laps!

Alternative form

Rope jump for one minute, then do a set of dumbbell swing.

Jump again for one minute and then do a set of dumbbells snatch.

Jump again for one minute and then do a set of dumbbell clean and jerk.

This is one round.

You can start with five to 10 rounds. When that gets easy, do rope jumping for two minutes.

Fat will melt off your body.

Points to remember

1. For fat loss, do three HOC workouts a week and a maximum of two regular weight training workouts.
2. If you want to build size or strength and also lose a little fat, do only one HOC workout a week.
3. Always perform HOC workout on an empty stomach (Take a serving of whey and green tea or black coffee 15 to 20 minutes before the session).
4. Drink plenty of water during the day.
5. Consume a top class whey protein supplement immediately after the workout.

High intensity interval training (HIIT):

High intensity interval training (HIIT) is an abbreviated form of cardiovascular training.

It's a boon to the modern-day trainee, who wants to lose fat fast.

Some experts are of the opinion that HIIT form of cardio is even beneficial during off-season – they claim that a trainee can lose fat while building muscle.

I would say that individuals differ and therefore there are persons who respond well to HIIT as well as steady pace cardio.

Reputable fitness guides say that the best way to do HIIT is in the ratio of 2:1.

In simple words, a trainee has to perform high intensity cardio for a minute and rest for 30 seconds. He has to repeat the process several times.

I put together such a plan based on an expert's suggestion and found that the results were amazing! The only problem is that HIIT form of cardio may not be suitable for persons who have joint or other kind of pain.

If your body is fine with such rigorous bouts, go ahead and try this workout.

However, ensure that your diet supplies plenty of protein and has lesser amount of carbohydrates and sufficient amount of essential fats. Drink plenty of water, train hard at the gym and sleep well.

Sample workout

Warm up on the treadmill by walking at a moderate intensity for five minutes. You can also warm up on the stationary bike, working at a moderate pace.

Now, run on the treadmill or pedal very fast sitting on the bike for 1 minute. You may then rest for 30 seconds.

This can be treated as one set.

Perform nine such total sets.

Finish it with a two-minute cool down on the treadmill or bike, working at a moderate pace.

How to find your muscle fibre type?

With an experienced coach by your side, find out your genuine one rep maximum for an isolation exercise for the muscle group you want to test, e.g. dumbbell curl. Now choose 80% of that 1 RM and do as many reps as possible with it.

If you can do only 4 to 7 reps with 80% of your 1 RM, you have mostly fast twitch fibers in that muscle. The reason is that fast twitch muscle fibers are strong but don't have lot of endurance.

If you are able to do 10 reps, then you have 50-50 split between fibre types.

If you can do 12 to 15 or more reps with 80% of your 1 RM, your fiber type is predominantly slow twitch. Slow-twitch fibres are not as strong but have excellent endurance.

Try this test on whichever muscle group you want and determine the fibre type.

To develop slow twitch fibre

If your fibers in a particular muscle consist primarily of slow twitch fibers, you will need to train that muscle with higher reps (12 to 15) taking less rest between sets and exercises and do more variety of exercises (high volume training.) Do remember that 12 to 15 reps mean choosing a weight that will allow you to do exactly that many reps to failure. Don't just take a light weight and do 12 to 15 without working hard.

However, slow twitch muscle fibers have a limitation. They cannot grow that much and so you should also do some lower rep training with heavier weights to maximise whatever fast twitch fibre you have in that particular muscle.

To develop fast twitch fibre

To maximize twitch fibre growth, do low to moderate reps, e.g. 4 to 8 reps, taking rest for 1 minute between sets and moderate training volume.

If your muscles have a reasonably even mix of fibres, you can evenly divide your training between lower-rep and higher-rep sets.

Mukesh Singh

CHAPTER 5

BODY TYPES

Not all persons respond at the same rate to physical training. You might have noticed that certain individuals are able to change their bodies almost week after week while some have to slog for months, or even years, to build a decent physique. Some individuals generally look lean and muscular while others look heavy and soft. Though success in bodybuilding is determined by a person's gene, understanding the basic classifications of body types – somatotypes – will go a long way in helping a person in building a good physique.

Peter Joseph Gnalian

Yogesh Sanan

Vipin Peter

Rahul Bisht

Sudesh Pawar

Ranjith Kumar

Tarun Dutta

Naorem Landan

Doctor William H Sheldon, MD, has classified the human body types as follows:

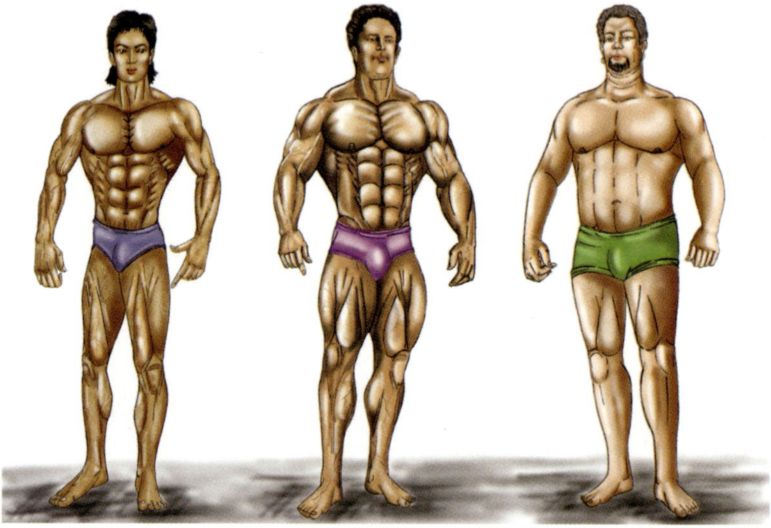

1. Ectomorph
2. Endomorph
3. Mesomorph

Allow me to present some general guidelines to be followed by persons belonging to each of the categories mentioned.

Ectomorph

Characteristics

- Generally lean
- Thin bone structure, narrow shoulders, small joints
- High metabolism

- Has difficulty in gaining weight

Training frequency

- Should not train more than two muscles in any workout (i.e., should not do more than three exercises for a particular muscle in a workout).
- Brief, abbreviated training routines preferable.
- Whole body routines, if used, should have only 5 or 6 basic exercises.
- Advanced champions can train each muscle very hard once a week; some changes can be made in training frequency based on recovery.
- Workout duration should not extend beyond 60 minutes.

Sets & Reps

- Use multi-joint or compound movements.
- Avoid isolation movements to the maximum possible level, at least until building some solid mass.
- Rep range should be from 6 – 8 using heavy weights.

Training intensity

- Increase weights whenever possible.
- Rest for at least 1 minute between sets.
- While training more than one muscle in same workout, rest for 3 to 5 minutes between each body part.
- Supersets, tri-sets and forced reps should be used

occasionally and not regularly.

Rest & Recuperation

- Should have more rest days.
- Eight or nine hours of sound, deep sleep needed each day.
- Taking a nap during daytime preferable.
- Do not train if the muscles are sore from previous workout.

Cardio

- Nothing more than two sessions a week.
- Work at lower end of target heart zone for 20 to 25 minutes per session.
- Use stationary bike or walk in brisk manner on the road or treadmill.

How to eat

- Eat 5 to 7 small meals every day.
- Eat once in every 2 – 2 ½ hours.
- Protein intake should be 30% of total calories.
- Carbs should be 50% of total calories.
- Fat should be 20% of total calories.
- Simple sugar consumption should be less.

General lifestyle

- Relax and unwind.
- Practice yoga and meditation.
- Do not indulge in other sports activities.
- Avoid tobacco, alcohol and drugs.

Endomorph

Characteristics

- Generally big with wide bone structure.
- Burns calories slowly.
- Gaining weight may be easy, fat loss difficult.
- Generally looks soft, which hides muscle gains.

Training Frequency

- Each muscle can be trained twice a week or once in three or four days.
- Choose five best exercises for each muscle and use three of them in every workout.
- Every fourth or fifth workout replace two exercises from the five movements chosen.
- Changing the order of exercises for a few workouts after every fourth or fifth workout will also help.
- A beginner can do whole-body routine for first two months and then adopt split routines.

Sets & Reps

- Train hard and heavy but in the range of 9 to 12 reps for upper body and 12 to 20 reps for lower body.
- Take minimal rest between sets (maximum 1 minute).
- Do not perform more than 9 to 10 total sets for each body part.
- If necessary, sacrifice a little weight to always help you complete the prescribed number of reps.

Raju Khan

Training Intensity

- Rest for no more than 60 seconds between sets.
- Advanced trainees can use techniques such as super sets, tri-sets, burns and giant sets.
- Drop sets technique can be used only on the last set of the final exercise for a muscle group, and only by advanced trainees.

Rest & Recuperation

- You need at least 48 hours between workouts for the same body part.
- You can get away with 7 or 7 1/2 hours of sleep every night.

Cardio

- Use joint-friendly activities such as brisk walking and stationary bike work.

Do a cardio workout 3 to 5

times a week with at least 30 minutes in the target heart zone.

- Performing cardio (20 minutes or a little more) after a weight workout ensures maximum fat loss.

How to eat

- Limit your intake of fat.
- Consume 2.2 gm of protein for every 1 kg of body weight.
- Avoid high glycemic index carbohydrates.
- Avoid late night snacking.
- Last two meals of the day should contain more protein and less carbohydrate.
- Avoid soft drinks, alcohol and tobacco.
- Drink several litres of water.
- Eat more solid food than drinking protein shakes.
- Protein shakes are best when consumed immediately after waking up and immediately after a workout.

General lifestyle

- Adopt a very active lifestyle.
- Unless your muscle gains suffer, participate in some kind of physical activity every day or just remain active.
- Rest and relax whenever necessary.

Mesomorph

Characteristics

- Solid bones yet some may have small joints.

- Long torso, wide shoulders.
- Naturally strong, a bit muscular always.

Training Frequency

- Can use both basic and isolation exercises.
- Variety of exercises can be used for better results.
- Alternate between 4 weeks of high intensity training and 1 or 2 weeks of low intensity training for maximum results.

Sets & Reps

- Total number of sets for each body part depends on the individual's recovery.
- Reps can be in the range of 8 to 12.
- At times, reps can be as low as 6 and can go as high as 25.
- Super fast recovery should not push you into overtraining.

Training Intensity

- Keep changing exercises, sets, reps, weights and techniques.
- Include heavy, moderate and light training days on a regular basis.
- Try techniques such as partials forced reps drop sets, pre-exhaust, post-exhaust, super sets and tri-sets.

Rest & recuperation

- You need 8 to 9 hours of sleep.
- Taking a nap during the day will also help.

- Do not train a muscle if it is not fully recovered from previous workout.

Cardio

- Train 2 to 3 times a week for 20 mins in target heart zone (this is excluding 5-minute warm up, 5-minute cool down).
- Work on treadmill, stationary bike or stair climber.
- Some persons can occasionally perform sprints for getting a good cardio while improving their legs.

How to eat

- Get 30% of your total calories from protein
- Carbs can be around 60% of your total calories
- Avoid junk food.

General lifestyle

- Listen to your body and train accordingly.
- Relax and build self-confidence.
- Proper planning can ensure phenomenal results.

A few words

Do all persons fit exactly into any one of these categories?

No!

Some individuals may have ectomorphic bone structure (such as tiny joints), yet respond amazingly well to training. Mr. Universe Serge Nubret from France is an example.

Some persons may have endormorphic component in that they get very smooth easily but gain muscle at an appreciable rate.

So, you have to make a general assessment of your body and use the guidelines offered here in a smart way.

Analysing the signals sent by your body and making changes based on that feedback is a must.

Initially, train under the guidance of an experienced and well-informed trainer to make your job simple.

The key to success lies hidden in a few words - observation, implementation and perseverance.

CHAPTER 6

TRAINING FOR VARIOUS GOALS

Xavier Joseph

In this chapter, I will discuss about training for various goals.

How to increase metabolism

If you are struggling to gain muscle or lose fat, it might mean that your metabolism is low. This simply means your body is unable to utilise calories efficiently and your endocrine system is not working at its best. This can be corrected by a simple system known as 20-rep squat programme. This squat should be a breathing squat. Inhale and exhale deeply a couple

Aneesh Raj

Vigneshwaran

Venkatesh

Nishant

of times, take in a deep breath for a third time, hold in your breath and squat down. Rise fully and exhale. This is one rep. Do 20 such reps. This is believed to help in increasing your metabolism. Don't just squat with a light weight. You have to eventually squat almost 1 ½ times your body weight, say experts. However, this might even take a couple of years or more to accomplish. So, gradually work your way up.

Along with this, do a few sets of bench press and chinning. Performing this kind of super abbreviated routine twice a week is believed to work wonders increasing your metabolism. There are experts who say that this programme can re-start the growth of your muscles that might have temporarily hit a roadblock. Your diet has to be spot-on to make this programme effective.

Focus on the rear

Modern science has proved that glute training has a major impact on improving metabolism. Glute weakness or the muscles being dormant affect the pelvic floor and lead to a whole gamut of issues. Man or woman, realise the value of glutes and start training them hard. You will be surprised to know that many of today's up-and-coming IFBB Pro bodybuilders do exercises like the barbell hip thrust and others for glute shape and health.

How to increase testosterone release

There is a super set combination which is believed to make this happen. Do a set of squats and immediately follow it up

Satyanarayana

Raja

Sudhakaran

P S Bhattacharya

Borun Yumnam

Daljit Singh

Rensu Chandran

If your progress is merely on the lines of "ok" and you still have a thirst to learn about more training methods, you might find the information given here useful.

Experiment with things carefully.

Less-than perfect advice

"Train heavy and train often" – this is the advice several champions offer hardgainers.

The truth, however, is that muscle growth is a very complex subject.

Why are some persons naturally stronger than others?

If the nervous system of a person is highly efficient, he can activate more muscle fibres while performing each repetition. This will mean that he can naturally be stronger and generate more force than the average trainee. He will be able to recruit more muscle fibres during each rep and, hence, lift heavier weights. This will him help to build denser, bigger muscles.

Researcher Arthur Jones used to call this "neurologically efficient."

Why are some persons naturally more muscular?

Some persons are genetically gifted. They might be neurologically efficient or might not be. They might also have more cells in their muscles, smaller joints (might be or might not), better appetite and better recovery ability from intense workouts. They might have less fat cells in the body and, those cells might also be well distributed all over the body and not bunched up in select areas. Their bodies might be efficient at burning fat as well.

Those who gain muscle at a reasonable rate might have a few or many of these qualities.

What is a muscle made up of?

Greater mass of muscle has three major components:

1. Myofibrils (known as contractile muscle), which form 20-30 % of the size of a muscle cell.
2. Mitochondria, which form 15-25 % of size.
3. Sarcoplasm (known as metabolic muscle), which forms 20-30 % size.

The remainder of muscle consists of the following:

1. Capillaries, 3-5 %
2. Connective tissue, 2-3 %
3. Fat deposits, 10-15 %
4. Glycogen, 2-5 %
5. Sub-cellular substances, 4-7 %

How to develop myofibrils

These allow the muscle to sustain maximum contraction for power and strength. To develop myofibrils, you have to do low reps (1 to 5 reps) through a full range of motion in a smooth, quick and strict manner.

Sarcoplasm

This is a protein liquid substance that fills and surrounds the cell. It contains enzymes and specialised structures to convert fats into sugars and sugars into energy. It also helps to metabolise waste products. Sarcoplasm or 'metabolic muscle' produces energy for muscles during contractions. The cardiovascular system helps to execute this job in an efficient manner.

Sarcoplasm increases proportionately with myofibrils and mitochondria. But they can be specifically developed by doing high reps in the range of 12-20.

Mitochondria

Mitochondria is part of cell containing genetic material and enzymes needed for cell metabolism, including those responsible for the conversion of food to energy.

Mitochondria can be developed by doing higher reps in the range of 15-30. They increase muscle endurance by increasing blood and oxygen supply.

Types of muscle fibres

Muscles that have a high percentage of myofibrils are called Fast-Twitch Muscle Fibres or White Muscle Fibres.

Muscles that have a high percentage of mitochondria are known as Slow-Twitch Muscle Fibres or Red Muscle Fibres.

No muscle, however, is made of completely one type of fibre.

Heavy training using low reps generally helps in building thickness in the muscles. Those who perform higher reps alone develop local muscle endurance but do not develop strength or size. But, integrating both type of work in a well-planned manner, according to an individual's needs, ensures success in building muscle, local muscular endurance and strength. There is a concept called periodisation and I have explained it in the chapter on training techniques.

Blood circulation and better growth

If blood circulation to a muscle is better, it has a chance of growing better. So, those who have an athletic or sports background start gaining muscle more easily.

Cardio care

Some researchers say that doing intense cardio immediately after hardcore training may hamper growth in certain cases, if not all. So if you are doing intense cardio after workouts and not growing enough muscle, stop that. Try doing cardio in a separate session and you might grow. Cardio performed after workouts may lead to overtraining in some cases. However, a moderate session of cardio after weight training is often considered the best for many people. Look for the feedback from your body and take a decision.

Fatigue products and growth

During intense workouts, the muscles accumulate fatigue and waste products like lactic acid. They help the body to release natural growth hormone.

Vijay Bahadur

Satish Kumar M

Wasim Khan

Rohit Shetty

Murthy

Gopinath

Manikandan

Prema Chandran

Satish Kumar

Surendran

considered worthwhile by the best of coaches. I have kept the explanation simple as this is no research manual.

I also believe that you needn't be familiar with the exact mechanism of each nutrient like a chemistry student to be a good coach.

Macros and micros

There are three macronutrients – protein, carbohydrate and fat. Vitamins and minerals are known as micronutrients.

Protein

Proteins are the building blocks of the body. They made of amino acids. There are 22 amino acids that make up different proteins. These amino acids are classified as non-essential, essential and conditionally essential amino acids.

Bio availability: According to experts, bio availability just means how much of protein can successfully pass through the gastrointestinal (GI) tract and reach the blood stream.

Protein digestibility corrected amino acid score (PDCAAS): This measures protein quality. PDCAAS depends on whether or not a protein meets the amino acid requirements of the body and how digestible it is.

Biological value (BV): Biological value is calculated as the ratio between nitrogen used for protein synthesis and total nitrogen absorbed. Eggs were rated with a BV of 100. Whey protein has a BV of 104, milk has about 90 and meats, between 70 and 80.

Types of protein supplements: Whey protein concentrate, whey protein isolate, whey hydrolysate, casein protein, milk protein, egg protein, soy protein and protein blends (a mix of isolate, concentrate with milk or egg, varies from brand to brand) are popular today.

Whey is one of the two major dairy proteins. It contains sufficient amounts of Branched Chain Amino Acids (BCAAs) such as Isoleucine, Leucine and Valine. These BCAAs increase protein synthesis (muscle growth).

Whey protein concentrates are those from which much of carbohydrates (lactose), water and fat have been removed. However, they still have some lactose. A high-quality whey concentrate may have protein percentage of 80. Concentrate is comparatively cheaper than isolate and hydrolysate which have very less lactose. Concentrates can be used almost till you are 6 weeks from a major bodybuilding contest, if the rest of your diet is super perfect. However, the last 6 weeks before a show, switch to isolate.

Whey isolates are those which have a protein percentage of over 90. Top quality whey isolates are believed to contain about 0.5% fat and 1% lactose.

However, a lot of care needs to be taken while making isolates. Any process of isolation that uses high temperature or low pH can affect the protein (denature it) and make the product less effective. Some years ago, there was a very popular process called ion exchange isolation process. It used acids, bases and electrical current to isolate whey protein. Heat was finally used to dry the product. Researchers eventually found out that these might affect the protein fractions.

The best modern process is very costly. These days, the best isolates are made using micro filtration. The most common process is called cross-flow micro filtration. It purifies whey under low temperature, low pressure and normal pH.

Whey protein hydrolysates or hydrolysed proteins are predigested (they are partially broken down into small pieces). They are quickly utilised by the system.

Casein protein – This is the main protein content in milk. A total of 80% protein in milk is casein and the remaining is whey.

Casein is absorbed very slowly by the body, ensuring a sustained release of amino acids in the blood for 6 to 8 hours. Casein is high in glutamine, which is the most prevalent amino acid in muscle tissue. Micellar casein is a type which is considered the best by many.

However, I personally don't recommend casein protein because of the lactose. Instead, take a serving of whey and some egg whites and almonds with it to ensure continuous supply of amino acids in the blood for hours, especially at bedtime.

Milk proteins – These are generally dried milk from which most of the fat and carbohydrate have been removed. It's definitely not the best for a person who wants to get to top shape.

Soy protein – This also has a lot of Leucine and glutamine.

Soy is also rated high on PDCAAS. However, soy contains phyto estrogens (plant estrogens). Though a lot of researchers have said good things about the benefits of eating soy, it may not be the best friend of a male bodybuilder trying to get hard, dry and muscular. I'm not asking you to totally avoid it. Just keep soy intake to minimum and avoid it during contest preparation.

Egg protein – This contains good amount of nine essential amino acids and arginine. Egg proteins are digested faster than casein. Eggs get 100% on PDCAAS.

Timing of nutrients

Upon waking up: Your body will be in a moderate state of catabolism. Consume a fast acting protein like isolate to quickly increase blood amino acid levels. This is believed to prevent the body from breaking down lean muscle tissue. And it also triggers anabolic action.

Before workout: An hour before training you will need whey protein, which is high in BCAAs. Some experts recommend a cocktail of whey and egg protein an hour before workout for a sustained elevation of blood amino acid levels.

Immediately after workout: A fast acting protein is required to repair and rebuild muscle tissue. Make yourself a cocktail of whey isolate with some glutamine and BCAAs. Adding of BCAA is being debated as many say the whey itself has plenty of it. If you consume enough protein, I don't recommend taking BCAA as a separate supplement and many top coaches accept this. (The BCAA acts as a switch to restart muscle tissue repair.) Glutamine is helpful in improving gut health and promoting recovery to an extent. It also is believed to volumise cells to an extent. Adding a top quality micronised (finely powdered) creatine monohydrate to this post-workout whey increases Adenosine Tri Phosphate levels and makes the muscles stronger for future working. Creatine also volumises cells and helps to gain muscle. There are various forms of creatine on the market and each one has an unique benefit. I prefer creatine monohydrate, which is the good old standard. I also do not believe in loading up on creatine. Having two servings of creatine a day with two of your meals is sufficient, according to one school of thought and I subscribe to that.

Some coaches say that a bodybuilder who used super-fast acting hydrolysate will benefit more because that kind of protein increases insulin levels, which is important to maximise transport of amino acids into muscle tissue.

One hour after workout: Solid food such as chicken breast, egg whites or fish are ideal. Have them with the right amount of complex carbohydrates, plenty of fibre and essential fats.

Between meals: When you are in a busy schedule and cannot eat 5 or 6 solid meals, make yourself a serving of a protein blend which offers whey isolate and egg to keep your blood amino acid levels high until your next meal. Add some essential fats to this.

Before bed: Mix yourself a serving of whey isolate and egg protein or take a serving of whey isolate and have a few egg whites and almonds with it.

This will prevent catabolism to great extent.

Best protein foods: Fish such as cod, Indian Salmon, tuna, seer; chicken breast; turkey breast; egg whites, whole eggs (if used in a sensible manner); lean red meats; paneer, tofu.

Carbohydrate

This macro is considered as fuel for exercise. The body stores carbs as glycogen in the muscles, liver and blood. When a muscle is glycogen depleted, exercise performance suffers. It's essential to refuel the muscles with glycogen for optimum exercise output.

Types of carbohydrates

Carbs are of two types – simple sugars, that are quickly broken down by the body and trigger an insulin spurt; and complex carbs, that are slowly broken down by the body. The unit that denotes the speed at which carbs are broken down is glycaemic index (GI).

Simple sugars or high-GI carbs are found in table sugar, fruit juice, milk, honey and flour. Simple sugars are generally consumed in small quantities, only when a quick refuel is necessary like immediately after running a marathon. Simple sugar leads to quick release of insulin, which is considered a storage hormone. Any person who wishes to stay in shape or lose body fat has to control his insulin output.

Complex carbs or low-GI carbs are considered best for maintaining good health and shape. It is the preferred source to keep glycogen reserves full. Nevertheless, unnecessary overloading of complex carbs might also lead to fat gain. Complex carbs are found in whole grains, whole wheat, sweet potatoes and whole oats. Take carbs only to fuel workouts and not to 'bulk up.'

Engineered carbs

Serious bouts of weight training deplete muscle glycogen. This has to be replenished before further physical activity, or else a person is sure to feel rundown. Glycogen replenishment, however, is not directly related to protein synthesis, some experts say. Nevertheless, post-workout carb ingestion is necessary for replenishing glycogen stores and also has a muscle volumising effect, according to many experts.

In general practice, many trainers ask bodybuilders to take simple sugars to quickly refuel.

The higher the GI, the faster the carbs are broken down and enter the blood stream and raise insulin levels. The highest GI food is glucose, with a score of 100. Fruit sugar or fructose rapidly restores liver glycogen and not muscle glycogen. A type of simple sugar known as dextrose was for long a favourite carb for post-workout shake.

A new type of complex carbohydrate, known as high

molecular weight carbohydrate (HMW), has been making waves in the recent years.

These kind of carbs, scientists say, get to the muscles significantly faster than simple carbs. These carbs do not cause bloating and reach the blood stream as fast as dextrose and restore glycogen much faster.

HMW carbohydrates quicken the rate of glycogen synthesis post-workout and increase the uptake of whatever vital nutrients are added to the drink. So, doesn't it make sense that champs add a lot of whey and creatine to this and drink it after a workout? Hold on, because many expert coaches say that whey protein, amino acids, and creatine all have a much lower molecular weight than HMW carb, and, therefore, can affect the total molecular weight of the solution and reduce the effectiveness.

To combat this, many suggest adding only small amounts of creatine and BCAA along with HMW carbs and consuming it immediately after a workout. Thirty minutes after this, a meal containing fast acting whey protein isolate and complex carbohydrates are recommended. A solid meal can be had later, they say.

Some of the popular HMW carbs are waxy maize and Vitargo.

My recommendation

I have found that HMW carbs are very highly priced and are out of the reach of many bodybuilders. Besides, I also believe post-workout carb refuelling might not immediately be necessary because an individual can take carbs and refuel even the next day an hour before working out. So, I personally recommend taking a whey protein isolate immediately after a workout with some healthy fats and 30 minutes later, a slow-releasing protein like egg whites and vegetable salad with fats. If you feel necessary, you may add a small amount of complex carbs to this solid meal and subsequent meals (based on your carb requirement).

Fibre

There are two types – soluble and insoluble. Both have a place in a healthy diet plan. Apart from vegetables, add psyllium husk, a soluble fibre, to your supplement plan without fail. It acts as a laxative, helps control cholesterol, blood sugar and blood pressure.

Fats

This macronutrient is very essential for several bodily functions, including the absorption of vitamins such as A,D,E and K. Fat is considered energy source and is responsible for maintaining healthy cholesterol levels (HDL vs. LDL).

There are two types of fats – saturated fats that come from animal sources, such as red meat and butter, and some of these foods should be consumed in low quantities or at least in moderation; and unsaturated fats, that come from fish, certain oils and nuts. Saturated fats are generally in solid state in room temperature and unsaturated fats are generally in liquid state in room temperature.

There are two categories of unsaturated fats – monounsaturated fats and polyunsaturated fats. Monounsaturated fatty acids are called Omega 9 fatty acids that are found in extra virgin olive oil and macadamia nut oil.

Polyunsaturated fatty acids are known as essential fatty acids (EFAs) because the body cannot produce them on their own. These EFAs play a major role in hormone production and muscle cell membrane repair. EFAs are very vital for muscle recovery and burning body fat. An individual who consumes very less EFAs will find it difficult to break down stored body fat and get into top shape.

There are two types of EFAs – Omega 3 fatty acids and Omega 6 fatty acids. The main Omega 3, known as Alpha Linoleic Acid, is found in high amounts in flax seed oil. However, that is not converted adequately into usable form of DHA and EPA by humans. The best source of Omega 3 fats is fish oil. Fish eat algae and convert the fat in that into usable form of EPA and DHA, which make them the best bet to get our daily Omega 3 fats.

The form of Omega 6 which is beneficial in improving health and reducing inflammation is Gamma Linoleic Acid (GLA), which is obtained from Evening Primrose Oil.

If a champion eats fish like tuna, cod or salmon twice or thrice a day and adds Evening Primrose Oil to his diet, he might not need EFA supplements. However, coaches like

Dave Palumbo suggest that a perfect ratio of Omega 3 versus 6 is essential for getting the best results in improving health and physique. They say that many people do not eat like that, and therefore, should take EFAs in form of a supplement that provides a balanced amount needed by the body. Dave says a hard-training athlete can take 3,000 mg of Omega 3 and 2,600 mg of Omega 6 in supplement form every day and be assured that there is enough amount of EFAs in his body.

My suggestion is, if you decide to go by Dave's recommendation, try out his diet too because the macro nutrients and supplement recommendation in his system form part of one unit and are made for each other. I have tried "Dave's ketogenic diet" on some of my competitor friends with good results. The bottom line is -- do not mix various diets and supplement plans.

Ideal protein-carb-fat ratio

There are many formulae to tell how macros have to be divided in an optimum nutrition plan. The most common suggests that a bodybuilder consume 25 to 30% of his calories from protein, 50 to 60% calories from carbs and 15 to 20% calories from fat. This is only a range and has to be tailored according to an individual. For this assessment, a person's Basal Metabolic Rate (BMR) or the number of calories needed to maintain the current body weight has to be calculated. The popular formula for men is to multiply the body weight in pounds by 12, and for women multiplying the body weight in pounds by 10.

More calories should be added in accordance with exercise and activity related daily expenditure. Now, this will be the number of calories needed to maintain the current body weight. If a person adds more calories to this number, he might start gaining weight. This is the grand old formula.

Labrada method

There are other ways to determine the ideal ratio.

According to world champion and well-respected coach Lee Labrada, a person who intends to reshape his body by losing fat and adding lean muscle simultaneously can consume 1 gm of protein per pound of body weight and 1.5 to 2 gm of carbs per pound of body weight. This is considered a very fine approach by many.

My preference

I personally prefer making this calculation based on lean body weight and not total body weight.

Add to this a couple of servings of fish, some almonds, extra virgin olive oil or coconut oil dressing for vegetable salad and Evening Primrose Oil, and your fat intake is also taken care of.

Fats play a major role in the production of certain hormones, act as lubricants to various parts and some types of fats also protect and repair cell walls. So, ensure that you get enough amounts of fats.

New supplements

The market is flooded with a variety of supplements like pre-workouts, intra-workouts and individual nutrients found in these products.

A good pre-workout supplement facilitates vasodilation (opens up blood vessels) and gives a vascular look and pump. This is made possible by a nutrient called nitric oxide, which is acquired by taking an amino acid called arginine. Pre-workout drinks have arginine, creatine and a few more such nutrients that give a pump and enhance mental focus. Intra-workout drinks have, apart from BCAA, a particular amount of citrulline malate, which gives a trainee energy for tough workouts. Taking such supplements as combined drinks or individual nutrients do have a place in a trainee's supplement plan.

As I said earlier, invest in solid food first. As regards supplements, take a good quality multi-vitamin/multi-mineral supplement, essential fats, fibre and a top class protein. These are the bare essentials.

You can add the rest based on your budget.

CHAPTER 9

TRAINING FOR COMPETITION

Riyas TK

Several up-and-coming bodybuilders are not very clear about how to exactly train for a contest. I have presented some general suggestions in this chapter to help such persons.

Training wisdom verbally passed on from the earlier generations have either been misinterpreted or not conveyed properly.

A case in example is doing high repetitions with light weight, taking minimum rest between sets. Though an increase

1992 Nationals

Jitender Dhillon

Tejender Singh

Sachin Dongre

aridoss

Kalaivanan

Sandeep
Duggal

Sandip Jadhav

Rohit Shetty

Sayanama Singh

Perumal Durai

Shyam Singh

Sathish Thampi

Ramakant Sharma

Sachin Patil

Harikrishnan

in repetitions can certainly help in training slow-twitch muscle fibres and enhancing the 'quality look' of the muscles, a drastic reduction in training poundage will lead to loss of muscle size. Some trainees may lose the hard, dense look of their muscles if they stop training with heavy weights and start high-reps with lighter weights.

Always remember that your body has been growing (or maintaining itself) in size, density and strength only because you have been challenging it with heavy weights. Once the "demand for growth in size and strength" decreases, the body will feel that it might not encounter challenging workouts again and, therefore, need not maintain the size.

So, the base of competition training should be almost the same as off-season training.

Workout suggestions

Here is how a routine can be put together while training for a contest:

1. Train each muscle twice a week or once in 4 to 5 days, depending on an individual's recovery rate. Some individuals can train each muscle even once a week – both in the off-season and contest training and see great results.
2. Begin with a basic exercise for a large muscle group. Using Pyramid technique, do 4 sets of 16,12,10 and 8 reps in strict style (no heaving or jerking).
3. As a second exercise, choose another basic movement.

Perform a medium weight warm-up set for 10 to 15 reps. If need be, perform another warm-up set. Then, choose a weight with which you can perform only 10 reps in strict style and get those 10 reps. Take a rest of 1 minute and try to do two more sets with the same weight. If you are not getting 10 reps but only 9 or even 8, it's fine. Just do them, and then rest for 1 minute. Doing multiple sets with the same weight is referred to as 'working sets' by some trainers.

4. As a third exercise, perform 2 or 3 sets of an isolation exercise with a weight that allows you to get 12 or maximum 15 reps. Rest for only 30 seconds between sets. Do a total of 2 or 3 such working sets with the same weight. Rest for 1 minute and go to the last exercise.
5. As the last exercise, choose another isolation movement and perform 2 or 3 sets of 30 reps, aiming for a good burn. Rest periods should be kept to a minimum. This concludes your workout for a large muscle.
6. For a smaller muscle, follow steps 2 and 3 as mentioned. Then, follow either step 4 or 5. This is because too much direct work on a small muscle during a calorific reduction phase (contest dieting) might lead to muscle loss.
7. Perform abdominal training twice or thrice a week, depending on your recovery. Choose one exercise each for the upper abs, lower abs, obliques and intercostals

and perform 2 to 3 sets of 15 to 20 reps on each one of them.

8. Use techniques such as forced reps in your workouts judiciously. Do not push beyond failure on all sets of all exercises. Every now and then, you can try drop sets on the last exercise for a body part. Many of these techniques can be tried even in the off-season. Just train smart while dieting so that you don't overtrain or injure yourself owing to calorific reduction.
9. Advanced competitors can combine opposite muscles using super sets or even the same muscles using compound sets. They can try giant sets or tri-sets. All these can be decided based on an individual's body, lifestyle, job profile and recovery.
10. Avoid cheating technique during contest prep to keep away injuries. Resist the temptation to swing the weights.

Cardio and fat loss

Cardio can be done either after workout (20 to 30 minutes) or as the first thing in the morning. Depending on an individual's recovery and fat loss, the duration and frequency of cardio can be decided.

As a general rule, 3 to 4 cardio sessions every week, each lasting 30 to 35 minutes, should be sufficient. If you choose to do cardio in the morning on an empty stomach, drink a cup of black coffee and then do your cardio. Never perform "fasted cardio" after drinking BCAA or whey as your body is not in a fasted state. Have a proper breakfast (with all nutrients) a little while after that cardio. Weight training can be done 5 to 6 hours later after eating 2 or 3 solid meals.

Cardio first, weights next?

When a bodybuilder hits the gym for a workout, he should ideally have some carbs in his system to fuel weight training. If he performs cardio first, his muscle glycogen (the stored form of carbohydrates) will get depleted. If he then moves to weight training, the muscles will not be able to train with heavier weights as the body would have little glycogen. Ultimately, his training poundage and intensity may suffer.

Weights first, cardio next?

Several coaches recommend doing cardio after a weight workout. This is considered a good idea because the body would have used all glycogen reserves for the bout with weights and when cardio enters the picture, it will immediately start burning fat. Complete your weight training within 40 minutes and then do 15 to 20 minutes of moderate intensity cardio such as walking. The entire workout should be over within 60 to 70 minutes. Lengthy sessions might affect recovery.

Cardio after leg workout

Anybody who wants to build size in the legs might find this approach to be a roadblock. This, once again, depends on the individual. So, the trainee who intends to play it safe can avoid cardio after leg workout.

These are some facts about cardio and every bodybuilder has to experiment and find out what approach suits him the best. There is no one-size-fits-all formula when it comes to serious bodybuilding. I know of several bodybuilders who do cardio twice a day and still retain lean muscle while some do not. So, please don't blindly imitate any champion and try to analyse your body.

What to do in the last 5 days before a contest?

By training hard and dieting properly, let us assume you have lost plenty of body fat and your muscles are showing lot of cuts.

By losing the subcutaneous water (found under the skin) and then loading the muscles with glycogen, your muscles will ripple with life on the stage and your veins with stand out like water hoses. Here are some suggestions on what to do in the last five days before a contest.

Glycogen depletion

Try as hard as you can, you will not be able to build new muscle in the last one week before a show. So, the best thing to do is to deplete the glycogen stored in the muscles so that the day before the contest when you cut water and start eating more carbs, the body will pull all that into the muscles and glycogen levels will increase dramatically. This is called "super compensation." This can make the muscle appear bigger, fuller and harder.

Your diet for the last five days should deplete muscle glycogen.

Let's assume that your contest is on Sunday morning and your weigh-in is on Saturday evening. Follow this protocol from Monday.

As the first step, keep your water intake high throughout your contest prep. If you have been drinking 7 litres every day all through your prep, keep it like this from Monday to Friday.

Train the muscles like what I have given below from Monday to Thursday or train them hard and heavy like you always did. Just avoid training to failure. This has to be decided based on an individual's body. Do not workout from Thursday. Let your body heal for 3 days.

Remember, there is no one-size-fits-all plan.

It's better to avoid cardio in this last week because doing it at this stage might lead to muscle loss and a loss of condition too.

Practice posing for at least 30 minutes every day. Stop taking stimulants in the last 3 days before a show.

Cutting water

Depending upon the individual, water cutting can start from Friday evening or afternoon. It will go on till Sunday morning. Do not drink water until the contest is over (on Sunday night). Some competitors start cutting water from Thursday, i.e., if they had been drinking 8 litres till Wednesday, they will reduce it to 7 litres on Thursday, 5 litres on Friday and 1 litre on Saturday. However, I personally feel that gradually cutting water might give the body a chance to adapt to less water. This is true in many cases, if not all.

So, my personal suggestion would be to totally cut water 1 ½ to 2 days before the show, which might trick the body and make it push out all water beneath the skin in anticipation that you are going to drink more like what you have been doing. This approach works the best for many competitors. Having a few sips while loading carbs might be of help to some competitors.

Carb loading

Amateur competitors who are very conscious of entering a particular weight category cannot afford to load for 3 or 4 days like pro bodybuilders who compete in open class contests. Amateur competitors have their own formulae for loading and here is one of them.

Carb loading is generally done after giving weight on Saturday evening. Some competitors who are dry, flat and need to fill out will benefit from loading carbs on Saturday morning or noon. I always recommend the competitor to pose for five to ten minutes and then load carbs. He can keep repeating this 'posing-loading' protocol once in two hours from Saturday morning or afternoon and continue it all through the night. I insist that the person keeps checking out his body before every meal to ensure that he has not started to hold water. If he has already started to hold water, it's better to stop loading and keep posing for 10 minutes once every hour. This will dry him out before the prejudging on Sunday morning.

Foods for loading

White rice and potato with some chicken or a few egg whites are the best. A little lime can be squeezed on the rice for taste. Competitors who are extremely dry eat apples and one or two ice-creams or even sweets in their loading regimen. I have seen such dry, muscular competitors eating a lot of sweets to quickly fill out. But I prefer loading with rice and potato with some protein like chicken or a few egg whites. On Sunday morning, get up and check out your posing. If you had cut water correctly (according to your body's needs), depleted the muscles properly and then loaded enough carbs, your muscles will look full, tight and hard. The veins will stand out prominently. Pose once or twice and eat a couple of more meals and you are ready to go to the contest. Carry puffed rice flakes which you can keep eating at the venue. Eat a couple of chocolates while pumping up and you will have enough energy.

Do not play with insulin for carb loading unless you have

an experienced medical team by your side. Messing up with insulin might lead to death.

Note: I have seen big champions eat a tonne of protein in their loading phase. But I don't understand this simply because protein cannot be loaded into the muscles like glycogen. If at all someone is extremely dry and feels that the sodium in the protein will enhance his appearance, he can add a some amount of protein like I said, but should not go overboard.

Sodium

I have also known champions sprinkling extra salt on their protein foods five or six days before the show and eliminating it in the end. I personally do not recommend this because unless the person is very meticulous and careful, the sodium-addition practice can ruin his condition on the day of the contest. Don't try this unless you have a very knowledgeable and experienced contest-prep coach working with you on this sodium-increase strategy. Do not try anything new in the last one week before a show.

Hariprasad

Here is a depletion workout routine, IF you choose to do it. Or else, train like you always did and stop working out from Thursday.

Monday

- Leg extensions 4 x 15
- Leg press 4 x 12-15
- Lying leg curls 4 x 15
- Dumbbell step-ups 4 x 20
- Standing calf raises 4x 15

Tuesday

- Lat pulldowns 4 x 15
- Bench press 4 x 15
- Lateral raises 4 x 12
- Tricep pressdowns 4 x 12
- Barbell curl 4 x 12
- Reverse crunches 3 x 20

Wednesday

- Barbell row 4 x 15
- Incline dumbbell press 4 x 15
- Bent over laterals 4 x 12
- Lying barbell extension 3 x 12
- Hammer curl 3 x 12

Thursday (Optional)

- Pulldowns 4 x 15
- Cable crossovers 4 x 15
- Dumbbell shoulder press 4 x 12
- Rope pressdowns 3 x 12-15
- Dumbell preacher curls 3 x 12-15

Diet during the last 5 days

Though there are several approaches to the last 5 to 7 days of a contest, here is one which is used by many competitors.

Don't change foods or try new foods in the last week of your prep. Just eat less carbs, less than what you have been eating in the past weeks of dieting. This is to reduce muscle glycogen. As you are not going to train extremely hard or till failure, the reduced carbs won't hurt you much. A 90 kg bodybuilder in top shape will not need more than 60 gm of carbs a day during these last five days. Those carbs should also be present only in the pre-workout and post-workout meals. I prefer the competitor gets these carbs only from complex carbohydrates. Rest of the meals should provide only protein, fibre and a small amount of healthy fat. (To avoid muscle loss, ensure that you eat at least 1 gm of protein for every pound of body weight, which means 2.2 gm of protein from every kg of body weight.)

Calculate how much carbs you need based on your body weight. These five days will deplete your muscles of glycogen so that once you start loading, they fill out dramatically. I know of competitors who stop eating even protein and totally starve all through Friday and Saturday to get ultra dry. This cannot be applicable to everyone and has to be decided based on the individual.

Weight reduction

To bring down the body weight, get drier and enter a particular category, serious competitors resort to extreme measures. Taking diuretics is a common practice, but might have serious consequences. There are herbal alternatives for diuretics, available in the form of food supplements. These are considered safe for a healthy individual. Following the label instruction and using such food supplements for the last 10 days can be beneficial to lose subcutaneous water and a little amount of weight. Don't play with sodium and potassium manipulation. The consequences might be very serious.

Sagar Pramod Mali

Methods

Apart from that, here are some methods our competitors adopt to bring down the weight.

Some competitors keep walking and walking (30 to 60 minutes), several times a day for the last one week before the contest. This will ensure that their body weight gradually comes down. Some of them might also stop working out and only keep posing every day. Some competitors also cut protein, which I feel, might not be a great idea. Stopping supplements such as glutamine and BCAA in the last one week may also help to reduce body weight, according to many champions. Creatine use is stopped the last two weeks before the contest.

Last-minute reduction

Some competitors wear three or four dresses one over the other and keep walking or running. This is generally done the last two hours before they register their body weight at the weigh-in. Some spray generous amounts of pain-killer (such as 'Relispray') on their body, put on 3 or 4 dresses and then go for running. This also helps to reduce the last ½ kg or 1 kg of water weight so that the person enters a lower weight category, they claim.

Conclusion

The steps presented here are what most of the competitors do. I do not endorse all of them. With enough experience or under the guidance of a knowledgeable coach, you can zero-in on the best methods for your body.

Some coaches do not change much in the last 7 days before a contest and do small manipulations, very carefully in a smart manner. As I mentioned earlier, there are several routes to a destination and some of them might be pretty good too. Go with a well-informed and qualified coach.

Maximum muscularity

Usually, training hard, dieting properly and staying lean in the off-season can ensure that anyone who begins a contest prep gets muscular without resorting to unconventional methods.

However, if some persons find it too hard to bring in maximum muscularity in the back, rear delts and thighs, I have seen their coaches recommend unusual techniques.

Here are some of my observations....

Supplementary training

After a thorough warm-up, the competitor will be asked to do four sets of chinning and bent over lateral raises (about 15 reps taking less rest and going for a pump) in the beginning of every workout on all days. The emphasis on chinning will be on slowly stretching the muscle and squeezing it at the top. This practice should not be done for too long as it might cause muscle loss. Trying it out 4 to 6 weeks before a contest might be sufficient for most competitors. This kind of training the muscle every day can be called 'supplementary training.'

Thigh separation

Some coaches recommend tri-sets for thigh workouts in the last three months before a contest. The thighs are trained two or even three times a week depending on the individual. The reps are always 10 to 12 and not low. Thigh muscles respond well only when a trainee does at least 10 reps, even in the off-season. So, ensure that you select the weight in such a manner.

Unconventional training

Despite all the effort, some competitors might not have enough muscularity in their thighs. I have seen some coaches adopt one of the following methods (I repeat, I need not endorse many of such measures) in the last 8 weeks to bring maximum muscularity in the thighs.

1. Some competitors perform 1,000 total reps of free squats (squats without weight) every day apart from a heavy leg workout done once or twice a week. This, they claim, brings good separation.
2. Some competitors perform 3 to 4 tri-sets of walking lunges, free squats or jump squats and duck walk every day apart from the regular heavy workout done once or twice a week.

Jaya kumar

3. Some competitors do 3 sets of leg extensions 500 non-stop reps each set using very light weight every day in addition to their heavy leg training done once or twice a week.

These methods may appear pseudo scientific, but have been adopted by many of our competitors. You can try anything only if it suits your body's recovery abilities. I personally do not vouch for the extreme methods.

Before we wrap-up…

Analyse your physique, train and eat accordingly, stay lean in the off-season, learn more about your body by working under a knowledgeable coach, listen to the body's feedback and be smart in adopting strategies.

There is plenty of information, all over the world and even in this book. Choose wisely.

Always remember what I said earlier -- there is no one-size-fits-all mantra.

Be smart and successful.

Chapter 10
The Good, the Bad and the Ugly

It all started sometime in the 1950s when anabolic steroids, discovered for saving lives of soldiers injured in wars, entered the bodybuilding scene.

I am not going to go into the history of drugs as it can be found elsewhere.

Bodybuilders initially were hesitant to try the first-ever developed steroid, which was an oral drug (tablet) called Dianabol. Those who tried the drug in the early 1960s took only one tablet a day (5 mg) for 6 to 8 weeks and just once a year for a major world championship. Over the years, more steroids were developed. Bodybuilders started to stack steroids (taking two or more steroids together) in the 1970s. However, they were reportedly taking it under a doctor's supervision and only for a couple of months in a year before a major contest. And steroids were not banned at that time and quality drugs were being manufactured by many well-known companies. In the 1980s, drug use started to increase as champions added 3 or 4 different steroids to their stack.

Some became irresponsible and kept taking drugs round the year. That it all ended up with serious health problems in later years is a different story. The next introduction on the scene was Human Growth Hormone (HGH or GH as it is popularly known). The use of this drug made bodybuilders extremely lean and, when combined in high doses with steroids, helped in building big, dense muscles. The next addition to the stack was insulin. This was meant to gain more freaky muscles by pushing all nutrients into the muscle cells. In between all this came diuretics such as Lasix, Aldactone and others that helped eliminate subcutaneous water before a contest. These diuretics can lead to severe mineral imbalance, thereby

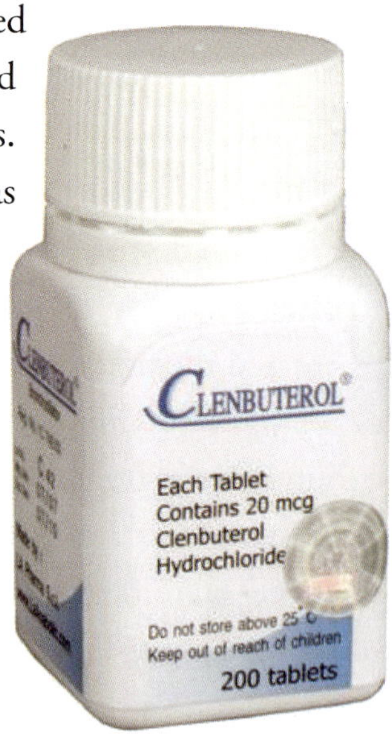

having a potential to stop the heart and kill the user then and there if abused.

Fat-burning drugs

The fat-burning drugs that became more popular were ephedrine and clenbuterol. These were incredibly powerful in raising the heart rate and helping the competitive bodybuilder on a diet burn fat like crazy. The initial combination of ephedrine, caffeine and aspirin (ECA stack) was super popular among users. When ephedrine was found dangerous and banned, supplement companies came up with herbal alternatives to mimic those drugs. These herbal supplements were safe only for the 100% healthy individuals as long as the label instructions were followed.

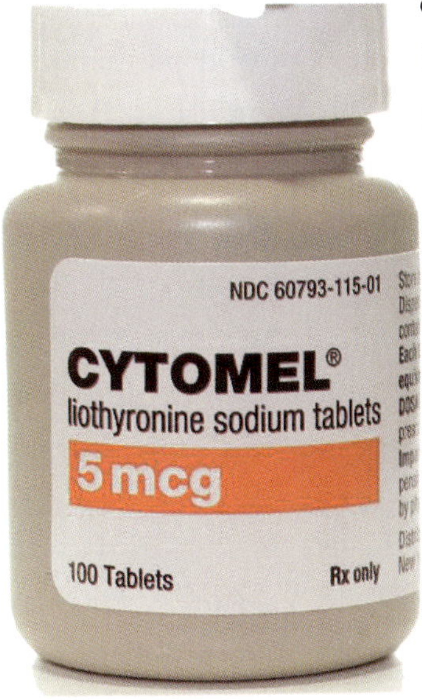

Clenbuterol, an asthmatic drug, was the next to be added to the ECA stack. Clen, a super powerful drug, had potential to do serious damage to the heart, especially when combined with lot of anabolic steroids and taken for a long time. A cocktail of Clen, ECA, HGH and powerful anabolic steroids started making competitors big, full and ripped beyond belief.

Thyroid and ripped glutes

The most powerful drug to be put in the stack was thyroid, especially T3. The other one, T4, was soon proved a bit inferior in making a person super ripped. Those who started using T3 lost the last layers of stubborn fat and started to show freakishly ripped gluteus muscle.

However, abusing thyroid had the potential to make a person permanently depend on it. Besides, reckless use of T3 could also break down lean muscle, which not many (till date) might know.

That is how the drug monster was fully born – ready to take on the world!

PGCL

PGCL (Cloprostenol Sodium) has been a recent addition to the fat-burning combo. This is a drug which was being used to trigger spontaneous abortions in animals. The side effects of PGCL include very frequent bowel movement and severe stomach ache. Prolonged diarrhoea and abdominal pain are likely among most of the users. Low energy, nausea, flu-like body temperature are common as well. PGCL also pushes out water from the body leading to a drier look, but the user will feel too tired.

There is a chance of localised site injection growth in many users and prolonged use leads to muscle and strength loss.

DNP

DNP (24 - Dinitrophenol) is, perhaps, THE deadliest fat-burning drug in the whole business. The drug breaks down stored body fat into heat. However, internal heat rises so much that the body literally gets cooked from within.

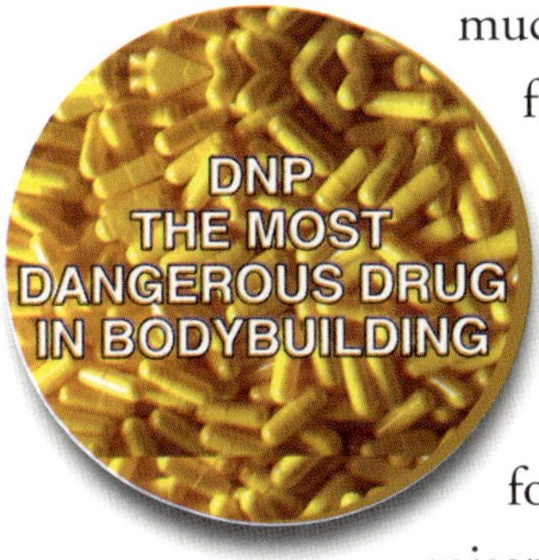

The common side effects include skin and body fluids turning yellow, excessive sweat and high fever. There is no medical treatment for DNP overdose and death will be miserable.

DNP increases the levels of Potassium and Phosphorous in the body and also causes kidney failure.

PGCL and DNP are among the nastiest of the lot and have to be avoided by all competitors.

Drug ban and UG labs

When governments saw the situation getting serious, they banned the sale of steroids and other such drugs over the counter. This, however, led to the emergence of underground labs (known as UG labs in short) that started to make all kinds of performance enhancing drugs. Many of them had no quality control measures and they still continue making drugs. They just keep making drugs under different brand names every now and then. There is no guarantee for their quality, potency and label claim. Many of them are sure to be under-dosed or made under unhygienic conditions.

Unfortunately, bodybuilders continued to take anything that would make them freakier and this practice has only got worse now. The federations tried to conduct steroid tests but gave up the idea later. The simple reason was that each and every steroid needed a different test and the cost of testing each competitor would run to thousands and thousands of dollars. So, some federations just tested for diuretics and very few tested for steroids.

'Bridging'

Bodybuilders slowly started to use mega stacks. Think about it – the early 50 mg to 200 mg a week for a maximum of 8 weeks steroid use became 2,000 to 3,000 mg a week. And, along with that, HGH, insulin and another powerful muscle-building hormone called IGF were all added. Many champions never came off the drugs even in the off-season. This gave them serious complications and there have been several deaths of champions since 2001. Some of them used to take 2,000 to 3,000 mg of steroids every week during contest season, but would continue taking 20 to 30 mg of some oral steroid in between two steroid cycles. This practice, which was later called 'bridging,' never gave their bodies a real break from drugs.

Protruding belly

The abuse of a cocktail of such drugs, especially GH, IGF and insulin, over a period of time made the internal organs such as the intestine grow. This kind of growth started to push the abdominal muscles outwards. To make their bodies grow to freaky proportions, the bodybuilders started eating huge meals once in 2 to 3 hours instead of eating small meals once in 3 hours. Eating so much of food made their belly hang loose and this aggravated the problem.

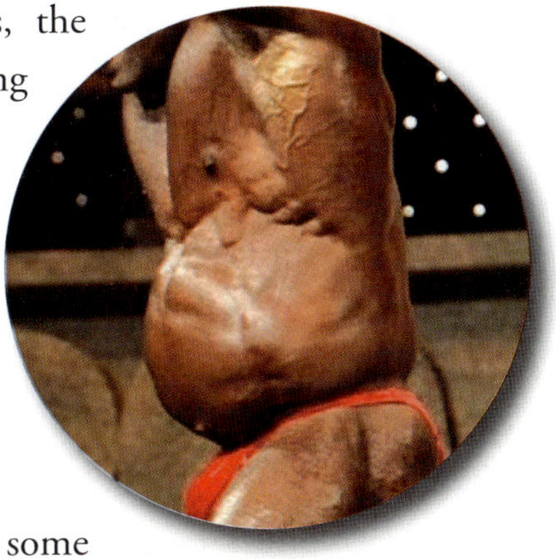

Reckless use of insulin, some experts contend, can increase omental fat accumulation under the stomach covering the intestines.

Finally, the use of monstrous weights such as 800 lb on squats and 2,000 lb on leg presses is also believed to be a reason for the belly growth, especially in people who abuse GH over months. All these made a bodybuilder develop a protruding belly though his body fat percentage remained very low and his abs deeply etched. This abdominal distention is being called bubble gut.

You might be able to see the joints grow and muscles like the arm might look short. The skin of some persons affected by this condition might also look unhealthy. The intestine grows to such an extent that it pushes the belly button (navel) outside and even if this is surgically corrected, the internal growth will make the abdominal muscles kind of split. The linea alba (abs) will develop a gap between them and eventually the gap will get bigger as the belly grows and protrudes. This has ruined the careers of so many professional bodybuilders.

Even as all these were happening at the international level, drug use started in our own country. Now, drug abuse is rampant even in India. There are signs of abdominal distention affecting even Indian champions and that is a very sad story.

Oily lumps

The mid 1990s saw the worst thing ever to happen to the sport of bodybuilding.

An oil came on the scene, which competitors started injecting into lagging muscles. Known as site enhancement oil (SEO), it would fill the gap and make the muscles look bigger. Such oils came in various names. A lot of pro bodybuilders and amateurs lapped it up and those who overdid it ended up with muscles that looked odd and unnatural with oil beneath them. For example, a biceps with too much oil would sport a pointed look even when the user stretches out his arm. Unseemly lumps on the shoulders, arms and calves were seen on lot of persons who did not realise that a person using this stuff needs to do it very carefully like a sculptor so that the gaps are filled without the region getting too big, pointed and ugly. This ruined the careers of many competitors.

This practice continues to have other serious consequences as well. There is always a risk of getting an infection owing to the presence of a foreign body inside the muscle.

There have been cases of people injecting SEO into a vein and stopping blood flow, and going almost to the doorstep of death.

SEO destroys real muscle?

Apart from such life-threatening risks, SEO use started proving counterproductive to the process of building and maintaining real muscle. When more and more oil is injected into a muscle, it blocks blood supply to that region, and eventually the person loses real tissue. I believe many of these oils, once injected, cannot be taken out of the muscle, or at least, not many know how to take it out.

Injecting oils is believed to be practised even in our country.

However, some expert coaches claim that a few types of oils are actually growth promoting as they are injected deep into the muscle and help in nutrient partitioning. Over a period of months, they claim, this leads to real muscle growth. As I am not an expert on this and have never tried this, I feel I shouldn't talk about this. Personally, I would say SEOs come into the picture only if you are a top IFBB pro competing at the highest level and have left nothing untouched to see maximum growth. Until you reach there, better not try SEOs, even if a few of them offer some extra benefit.

Site injection

There have been cases of competitors doing site injection – injecting certain steroids into various lagging muscles believing that they might lead to some localised growth. I have never injected steroids or oils for such a purpose and I am not qualified enough to talk about this topic.

I belong to the old school of thought which says that the best way to gain lean muscle is to eat right, train hard and rest enough.

Drugs and risks

It is very sad that so many people have now become coaches just because they know how to combine drugs and make a client muscular.

As I said in the earlier chapters, I was not a natural

bodybuilder. However, I am a person who believes that there is a line between use and abuse of drugs. A lot of coaches now give mega drug cycles just because they want their clients to look freaky and win titles. I am clearly against teenagers taking steroids and also condemn the abuse of a cocktail of drugs.

Many of the so-called coaches do not know the serious consequences of drug abuse and young, impressionable minds get carried away by what they say.

When such messages are posted on social media, I am saddened to see responses from young people that they prefer to die in their 30s after winning big titles rather than living with smaller titles and good physiques till they are over 70.

I am at a loss of words and unable to write any further on this.

How to tackle the drug menace?

Whenever I write articles in magazines about the serious health consequences of anabolic drug abuse, naïve readers, who most often are new to the sport, ask me when and where natural bodybuilding contests (city, district and State-level competitions) are organised so that they can participate. The bodybuilders who have previous experience of competing several times and are aware of the current scenario criticise me, saying that I am trying to mislead my readers by painting a picture of a dream world because there aren't going to be any genuine natural contests. Why is it so?

Let us try to analyse the situation.

Natural contests

There are some bodybuilding associations at the world level that test the competitors for steroids. It really seems to be a genuine effort as many of the competitors flexing their muscles there look pleasing and are far from freaky. Some of the rules enforced seem to be strict, so I guess many of those associations do test their athletes. But I honestly don't know if every one of these associations test for all steroids, or at least, the most popularly used, HGH and Clenbuterol. Besides, how are the associations going to test for fast-acting steroids that are in and out of the system within a few days? Are the competitors randomly tested round the year? If yes, it is truly amazing and I bow in respect to them.

Reg Park

With all these points in mind, let us look at the scenario in India. I don't think there are that many drug-tested competitions being held in our country. If at all an association wants to test its athletes, the cost of tests for even one or two steroids will be pretty high. That being the case, can the associations afford to spend lakhs of rupees on drug tests alone? Can the competitors be tested for the widely used steroids if not all drugs? Will the competitors finishing in the Top-5 in every weight category be tested? The cost factor is the biggest roadblock to implementing foolproof drug testing at all contests, whether in India and even abroad.

All cheats? No

Wait a minute. I am not saying that all the persons competing in such contests the world over are cheating. No. Many of them might be 100% drug free. I just want to stress that drug testing is a super-huge thing for any country and certainly not as simple as what many people think it is. So, there are going to be some persons who might cheat and get away. And implementing testing in a country like ours is close to impossible. That is my point.

Solutions

Well, after all this, shouldn't I offer a solution or at least give suggestions to make the scenario better in our country? Here are a few points to ponder:

First and foremost, we have to realise that competitors are definitely going to be doing whatever it takes to be competitive. So, there is no point in blaming them or merely scaring them about the drug issue. A little bit of serious thinking will clearly tell us that nobody would really want to die or suffer from multiple-organ problems that might manifest in the later years owing to drug abuse.

Competition standards

The bottom line, therefore, is that competition standards should be brought down. This is a very practical step that all the federations can take. The federations can send circulars to all State and district federations instructing their officials to take the judging standards back to what they were 20 years ago when drug use was less.

Young abusers

Experienced judges, trainers and competitors will clearly be able to spot a young person who has suddenly jumped onto the scene from nowhere and is looking freaky. This cannot be accomplished without taking loads of drugs. A person who has been training and competing for five or six years and gradually improving (taking only a small amount of drugs and not abusing his body) will show muscle maturity and thickness which an upstart will lack. The judges can start by placing young new freaks much lower and telling them to their face that their drug abuse has brought down their placing. Not all new competitors can look extremely ripped, dry, vascular and yet thick within a couple of years of training.

If a person truly has amazing genetic potential to look so freaky within a few short years of training, he would very soon look much different from even those who have been competing for some years. These are the persons who can win world championships and become top professional bodybuilders. However, it is not every day that you come across such potential. Please realise that a majority of the newcomers who suddenly and dramatically transform their physiques are heavily juiced up. The extreme muscularity and dry conditioning, usually seen only after years of competing, cannot be achieved by a new kid without relying a lot on drugs. So, those who decide the placing at the contests and the federation authorities should be firm in their decision of marking down freaky young newcomers.

Senior abusers

This can eventually be taken one step further. Even the senior athletes who look like freaky monsters with protruding bellies can be placed a few spots lower. This will force the competitors, seniors and juniors, to think.

The seniors do not need loads of drugs to compete. Years

I personally feel that this is indeed taking things to the extreme.

of hard work, proper eating and experience can help them look really good with minimal drugs. They are forced to rely a lot on drugs only to be competitive with the others who abuse drugs.

Things might change if the monsters among them are also marked down. The seniors might stop taking too much of drugs and start taking only a small amount while getting ready for a show. They will, therefore, lack the freakish look. But they will still be good enough to win any big title. Juniors might stop abusing drugs on seeing their favourite seniors being placed low because of drug abuse.

This will make the sport more appealing to the common man (and women too) who might not like to see monsters with their bellies sticking out and extreme vascularity. This might gradually move the game up on the popularity ladder.

Will it be implemented?

Such steps by judges and officials will certainly be met with serious opposition.

The persons enjoying power need tremendous determination to take such steps and remain firm on not giving up. If this is implemented 100% over a couple of years, drug abuse will certainly come down. Competitors, once they realise that they need not resort to extreme measures, will be happy to scale down the drug use, more so because they will be saving plenty of money spent on drugs.

Sports quota jobs

Bodybuilders in our country are given government jobs in sports quota only to encourage them. However, the present day standards are very high and the extreme steps taken by many young people, if not all, are sure to cause major health problems as the years go by.

If a person takes a lot of GH and steroids regularly for 4 or 5 years for placing well in his job-related contests or nationals or even to win contests to qualify for a job, it will be no surprise if he develops serious health issues before he turns 50. So, bringing down the standards will ensure better health for all those who train for getting government jobs.

All these suggestions will definitely improve the situation and make the sport much healthier, if not totally clean. I personally feel it is too much to expect for a total clean up in the sport. Taking such sincere steps towards stopping drug abuse is much more practical.

My message

With all that said, what is my stand on drug use?

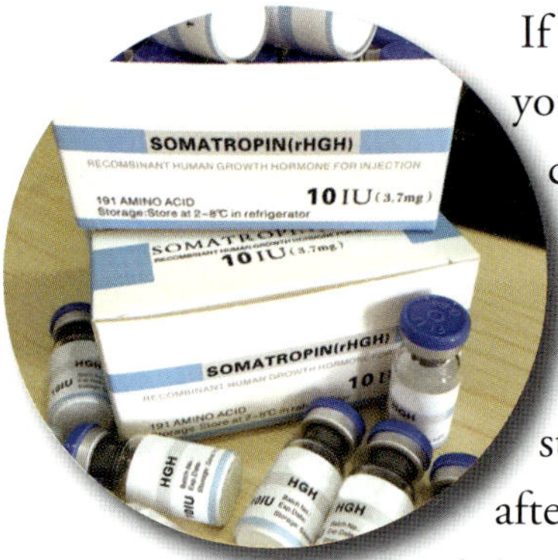

If you want to stay natural, I salute you for the decision. Please stay clean for a lifetime and keep competing even with those who are doing drugs. Your physique, though might not be freaky, will stay good and healthy for years after you retire, provided you keep training smart and eating right. You might even win some titles, which depends on an individual's genetic potential.

Want to try drugs?

If you want to take the risk of trying drugs, always educate yourself, think well and decide.

Teenagers should not use steroids as it might fuse growth plates in the bones and affect height growth. Besides, teenagers might get addicted to performance enhancing drugs at a very early age and might feel lost without the use of drugs eventually.

Not for first few years

Any beginner should not use any kind of drug for at least 3 to 4 years of his initial, basic training. He should first lay a solid foundation of muscle mass and start looking like a bodybuilder with enough growth in all muscle groups. He should compete in smaller contests naturally using only food supplements and try to place well.

Analyse your potential

After making significant progress as a natural competitor in city, district and State levels, he can think whether he needs drugs to go further. A clear analysis of his genetic potential and progress made with systematic work will tell him how far he can go as a competitor.

Drug use is an individual's decision, an educated decision taken by a mature adult, let me add. If a person aged over 21, after 5 or 6 years of initial natural progress, feels he might need drugs to go beyond national level contests, he has to first ensure that he his family has no history of health issues. He should then seek an experienced and reputable contest prep coach and learn more about drugs, their harmful potential, precautions to be taken, post cycle therapy (PCT), medical tests to be done every now and then, and on how to keep the cycles short and infrequent.

No mega stacks

A person shouldn't stack too many steroids in his very first cycle and should also stay away from harsh orals. If a person decides to take the 'juice' (performance enhancing drugs), it makes sense to take a couple of compounds in moderate doses and keep the cycle short.

Taking too powerful drugs in the very first cycle and that

A woman will never look this muscular unless she uses performance enhancing drugs.

too in high doses might force a person's body to stop responding to drugs very quickly. This might force him to add more drugs to his stack in the subsequent cycles and increase the doses, which all translates into harsh side effects and serious health complications.

A first-time user should not try extremely powerful drugs such as T3, Clen, insulin or HGH. Please resist the temptation and keep your cycle short, simple and sensible.

Less is good

There have been world champions who have taken very less drugs infrequently and won the biggest of titles. Arnold Schwarzenegger has admitted to taking steroids during his competitive heyday. However, the doses he took were very less and the cycle was just once a year while getting ready for the biggest world championship like Mr. Olympia. Check out his video while he prepares in 1975 for his sixth title defence. You will be astounded to see his amazing condition which was achieved with very moderate doses of steroids (much low when compared to the present-day monster stacks used by many novices) and without the use of Clen, insulin, IGF or HGH. So, you don't necessarily need a truckload of awful stuff to look great.

Drugs cannot compensate for genetics

And remember that no amount of drugs can make a person with little genetic potential win a Mr. Olympia. If drugs were all that made champions, then the richest man who can afford to live on mega stacks and super supplements will be No. 1 in the world. This is certainly not the case and don't step into the quicksand of monster stacks.

Do remember that the extreme rigours of contest training and dieting for several years might be stressful to the system. Job and family related stress and financial pressure might add up to that load. Throw in drug abuse and you have a surefire recipe for disaster. Always be sensible and don't go to the extremes.

Abuse need not necessarily mean immediate death. It might immerse you in physical and mental agony for years until death comes calling.

So ditch that 'heroic' talk of dying like a warrior because abuse is only going to make your death pitiful.

Being smart, in every sense, is expected out of you because it is YOUR life and you live only once.

Watch out for fakes

Everyone who seriously hits the weights with the intention of getting really fit, reshaping his body or building muscle can be seen carrying a shaker to the gym.

Food supplements are really helpful and I am happy that a lot of people are aware of good products coming from reputable companies.

But not many buyers are serious about wiping out fraudsters who dish out fake supplements and rob people of their hard-earned money.

Early history

Food supplements coming from abroad appeared on the scene in India sometime in the mid 1990s – that is what I am being told.

People realised that food supplements were getting more and more popular and it was becoming a huge industry. This might have prompted some persons to initially import small quantities of supplements from countries like the U.S.

With the acceptance of those products in India, more people turned their attention towards bringing supplements from abroad, perhaps not paying too much import duty to the Customs Department – through friends in small quantities or smuggling.

Olympia Jai

Monotosh Roy

M Durairaj

Durai Shankar

Albert Paulraj

Manohar Aich

G Balan

Sunil Patro

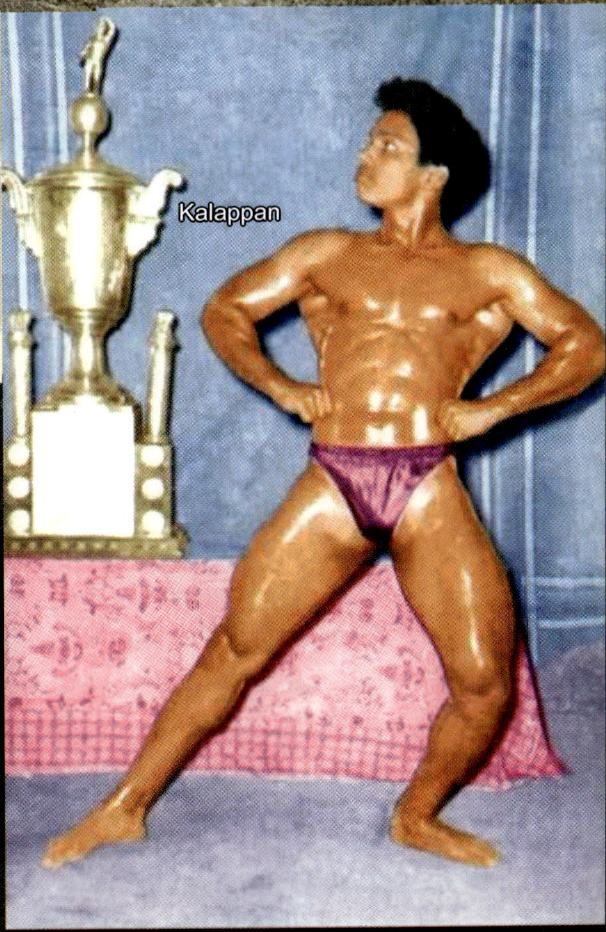
Kalappan

K V Thirumalai

fat and pharmaceutical diuretics such as Lasix, Aldactone, Diazide and others for losing subcutaneous water before a contest.

A natural bodybuilder is free to use whole foods and food supplements such as protein powders, BCAA, weight-gainers and pre-workout and intra-workout powders that do not have certain ingredients banned by select sports federations. A natural bodybuilder can also use fat burning supplements and herbal diuretic supplements that do not contain certain banned ingredients.

Success rate

With all these said, you might ask me if a person can really build a great physique under such conditions.

My honest answer is "Yes." A 100% natural bodybuilder can indeed build a great physique. However, it is going to take him lot of time – anywhere between 5 and 20 years to achieve it. Depending on a person's natural, God-given muscle-building potential, the time needed to build a great physique will vary. Nevertheless, it is possible.

Requisites

With that assurance of success, let us see what are the requisites or what all a trainee has to do to succeed as a natural bodybuilder:

1. A natural bodybuilder has to be meticulous in his diet plan and eat once in two-and-half to three hours. Each meal should be specifically made for the individual's

body and have enough amount of macronutrients.

2. Food supplements should be used only at the right times and only when they are needed. A protein powder cannot ideally replace a meal of whole food protein sources and complex carbohydrates. In simple words, do not take protein powders just because it is easier to consume than cooking chicken breast or fish or egg whites.
3. Cheating in diet should be kept to bare minimum and the trainee just cannot afford to miss a meal unless he gets sick and is told by the doctor to avoid heavy protein foods for a few days while on treatment.
4. Workouts should be intense, yet smart and not lead to overtraining.
5. The trainee should concentrate on the basic exercises such as squats, deadlifts, barbell row, bench presses, shoulder presses and power cleans. He should use barbells and dumbbells and the use of machines should be kept to a minimum. The machines he can use are triceps pressdown machine, calf raise machine, lat pulldown machine and leg press and leg curl machines. Other machine exercises can be brought in only after the trainee has gained 10 kg of solid muscle and needs variety. This situation might arise after a few years of regular, systematic and planned training and eating.
6. The focus should be on genuinely feeling the muscles stretch and contract while working out and

of training and start losing size and hardness. Please realise that you need to do whatever you did to build that muscle, even while dieting. However, when you cut carbs, your strength levels might go down. So, instead of totally stopping the use of heavy weights, just reduce the reps by one or two and still do that heavy work. For example, if you can squat 140 kg for 10 reps in the off-season, do that 140 kg even while getting ready for a show. But, do 8 reps instead of 10. If you can still do 10, do it as long as you can. Just don't do too many sets and make adjustments every workout based on how you feel that day and on your recovery.

Smart training is what you need. Don't train beyond failure.

Techniques to follow

You can try various training techniques and training splits, all of which you might have done in the off-season, even during contest prep. Many of the techniques and training splits found in *Mind, Muscle Moksha* can be used both in the off-season and while preparing for contests. They are not just for the athletes who take drugs. These techniques and splits can be smartly used by a natural bodybuilder too, based on his recovery. Once again, you have to be smart and listen to your body's feedback to pick and follow all these principles.

Winning naturally

Can all of you win a contest naturally? The honest answer is 'No.'

KV Iyer

You don't need a rocket scientist to tell you this.

The person who has the best genetics to build the most beautiful body and who has really achieved it will be the winner. However, those who have trained smart and been following all what has been said here for years will finish a close second or third behind him. It is, nevertheless, a wonderful achievement and cannot be ignored at all.

Just forget genetics and start doing all that has been said. Eat all those meals 6 to 8 times a day, train like what I said and keep repeating these steps for years. Patience, perseverance and commitment are the words that you need to keep in mind. You will be an awesome natural bodybuilder.

Realisation

One final advice would be this – natural or otherwise, think about competing only after you have built enough muscle for your height. Don't start a contest preparation just because you want to compete or just because you have trained for one or two years.

Compete only if you have built enough muscle and are ready for it.

CHAPTER 12

MIND, THE POWERHOUSE

Almost every day you hear about the 'power of mind.' This has been stressed so much that many have actually developed an aversion to this phrase. Though this 'mind power' has been exploited too much in today's commercialised world, it is indeed a super-powerful tool to get you the most of what you wanted, if not all, and keep you happy for a lifetime.

Read on and I will explain several scenarios which you might encounter in your life. If you really know how to use your mind

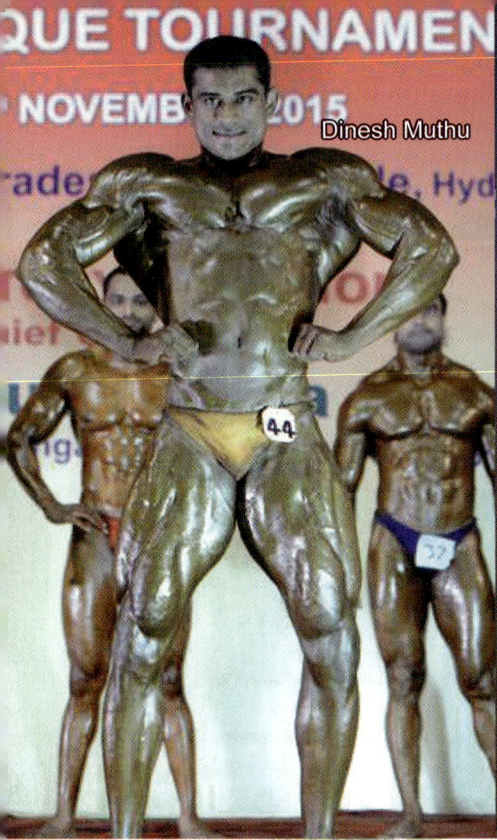

Dinesh Muthu

Virender Malhan

Ponmudy

Anthony Kumar

Vinit Marwaha

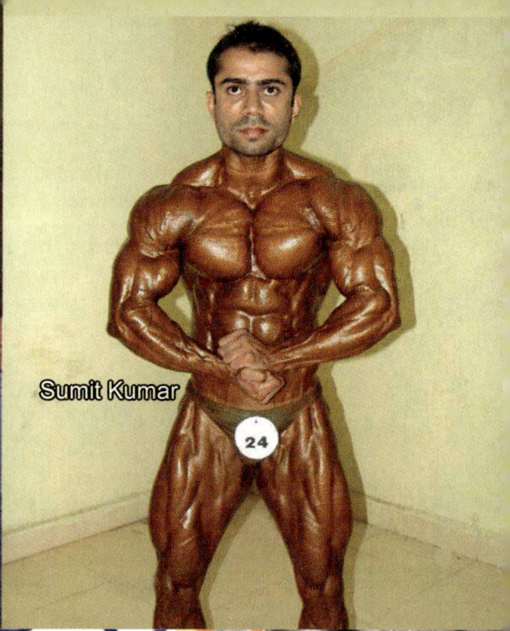

Sumit Kumar

R Munusamy

to plan and tackle any situation, you are sure to make it big. Here is the most common question that is asked by novices…

How do I become a champion?

The techniques, diet plan and strategies given in *Mind, Muscle, Moksha* take care of the guidance part, especially in a manner that is second to none. However, there are a few more things one has to keep in mind if he or she desires to rise to the top as a physique competitor.

Goal setting

You have to first analyse your physique and break down your goals into two – short-term and long-term. This is the most important part and the one who fails in this is sure to suffer in the longer run. You might find this mentioned somewhere else in this book too.

If you lack muscle mass, set yourself a goal of adding 4 to 5 kg of lean muscle in the next 12 months. This is a long-term goal.

If you have been training for a few years but lack good thighs or arms, set yourself a goal of adding ¾ inch on your arms in the next 4 to 5 months or 1 inch on your thighs in the next 3 to 4 months. A systematic, planned approach to workout, diet and supplements is needed to make this happen. A poorly-planned approach will not yield results. Concentrate on the basics while simultaneously paying attention to specific areas only to the extent needed. If you are a physique competitor or woman athlete, set yourself a short-term goal of reducing an inch around your midsection and waist in the next 3 months and adding an inch or so around your shoulder region (by growing your side deltoid). Men can try to get tighter and a bit wider in the region around the lower chest and the area where the back meets the rib cage. Aim for an overall different look by the end of 12 months and keep it going. That will be a long-term goal.

When to enter your first contest

Figuring out this is very tough. If you are a bodybuilder, you should look pretty solid with lot of muscle in all the muscle groups before you actually plan to step on a stage. As an example, if you stand around 5 feet 8 inches but weigh only a ripped and lean 70 kg, you are going to look small on the stage. A muscular body weight of at least 80 kg is essential for you to look decent, if not big. Also see to it that you have enough muscle in all the areas like legs, shoulders and arms.

What prize to expect?

Unless you have great genetics, you might not win a top 3 slot in your very first contest. There are many great champions who did not win any prize in their first few contests but went on to become greats. Start competing because you love it and keep learning to get better as you do more contests. The contest prep, when repeated frequently in the first 2 or 3 years of your competitive career, will fine-tune your physique and refine it for future victories. Just ensure that you don't end up abusing your body and that is the most important thing to keep in mind.

Off-season goals

Don't go crazy and gain a lot of weight in the off-season. Gain predominantly lean muscle, do not develop 'spare tyre' around your waist and do not allow your abs to completely disappear. If you don't rush to gain too fast and keep it slow, you will gain lean muscle and very less body fat and this is the ideal way to become a great body building champion.

How to be a good trainer/coach?

What I said until now is related to your planning. There are a lot more places where you need to be careful as far as the mind is concerned because it is like a raging steed and needs to be steered in the right direction. This will ensure that you succeed not only as an athlete but also a coach.

Now, I will present a few scenes that you might have seen in gyms. If you are a trainer or aspire to be one and be successful in it, avoid the mistakes I have mentioned.

Stop ridiculing natural trainees

I have seen this happen just too often. Young and arrogant body builders, especially novices, when given a job as trainers, ridicule clients who wish to stay drug free. The so-called trainers do this to young kids who come to the gym to lose fat or build a decent physique. That these kids have no intention of competing and luring them to performance enhancing drugs is criminal. If you have won a few titles, feel good about it and take pride in it. That is fine. But don't put clients on drugs as soon as they start training and don't psychologically cause damage to them by making fun of their decision to stay genuinely drug free. Instead, make them a perfect diet with all essential food supplements and ensure that they train hard, yet smart.

Don't mess up

I have seen trainers who read a lot written by the greatest coaches and keep trying something new on their client during every single workout. This is not needed. Muscle confusion technique might work wonders on an advanced champion. But, your average client who desires fat loss or aims at looking good need not benefit from this. Don't do funny experiments or don't overdo the techniques because you might mess up things and waste time.

The best technique?

I have seen trainers who claim that the training technique propounded by X or Y alone is THE best. I am sorry, there is no one single system which can be promoted as THE best. Almost all techniques presented in *Mind, Muscle, Moksha* work well. It is all about how you correctly judge a client's necessity and pick the right ones in their training phase. So, you, as a trainer, should be smart and not feel that you have learnt everything and that yours is the only way to train.

Internet guru

Young and impressionable minds rely too much on the internet and end up doing ridiculous things. Now, I also see a lot of videos giving wrong and incomplete information. My sincere suggestion is to learn only from pioneers and world-class coaches and not from those who have exploited the social media. There are some big names in India and several on the international scene. Identify them, observe them, analyse their work, learn from all that, adopt and improve and keep doing it. Over a period of time, your knowledge will grow and help you take the right decisions. That is when you are ready to become a coach. You don't become a coach by watching a few videos or entering chatrooms or learning drug cycles and winning a few titles.

Balakrishnan

Analyse limitations

There are some trainers who refuse to analyse the limitations in their clients. If a client is unable to do squats, find out what makes it so difficult for the person to do it? Is it an issue with the knee or tightness in the quadratus lumborum or is it due to the glutes not firing enough or too much of tightness in the hips?

The answer can be any one of these or more than one of these too. Unless a trainer finds it out and sets it right, the client will not be able to do a squat painlessly. A trainer should not blindly force a client to do the basics (even though they are essential) without addressing the issues.

Body language

Many young competitors earn a bad name by and large due to their body language in the gym. This is enough to do you more damage and ensure that you get only a fraction of the success that you are worth. Let me add here, your words also earn you respect. Be warm and respectful when you address any client. Never talk ill of anyone, including your competitors or rivals. This will help you big time, I promise you that.

Avoid blind imitation

If you are a trainer, stop blindly imitating your hero – in training or diet and drug use. Never blindly use those ideas while working on a client. Culture your mind in such a way that it appreciates the law of individual differences. One man's formula for success might be another's recipe for disaster. Be smart and your mind must be taught to understand and accept this fact.

Hold back emotions

Never show your stress or emotional turmoil to your clients. A person might be coming to a gym to get a break from his or her monotonous and stressful life. If you, a trainer, who lets stressful vibrations and emotions permeate to the client, the person is not going to continue using your services. Leave your emotions and stress at the doorstep of the gym. Make the floor a place only to get a great workout and that will enhance the mood of your client. A happy client lets out a lot of positive vibrations and those will make a trainer feel relieved of his stress and content. This is a sure-fire technique to being a successful trainer.

Client is no ATM

I have heard a sad story from several people. There is a wide condemnation that competitors, when hired as trainers, dump unnecessary supplements on their clients and earn profit for meeting their expenses. There have been accusations that some competitors pester their clients for sponsorships to compete. Though I have tremendous respect for competitors, I don't approve of such practices. Such people are doing more damage than good to our field. If your services are good and you are warm and courteous to your clients, they themselves will be glad to help you meet your expenses, at least to some extent. Instead of trying to exploit your clients, work hard and impress them by your ethics so that a couple of them are glad to help you. This approach will earn you respect and long-term success while those who adopt the wrong practices will lose clients. You have to make a smart choice.

Train, not treat

Tell your mind clearly that unless you are a certified medical practitioner (doctor), you should not treat the complaints of your clients. Refer them to a good doctor or sports therapist. Always work in coordination with a couple of such persons so that your client gets the best guidance and your practice and clientele grow. A good trainer should not don the role of a doctor, unless he is academically qualified to be one.

Selfishness is cancer

When you always think only about YOUR workout and diet, you might actually become selfishness personified. I have seen young athletes refusing to do even minimum work at home, saying they can't afford to miss a workout or meal. If your contest is next week, then this makes sense. But, if it is 6 months away, doing a few household chores now and then for your parents is part of your duty. If you do that, your parents might support you in your pursuit. Don't be too crazy or selfish. Same is the case when it comes to your behavior with your life partner and kid. Spend time for them and make them feel that you love them. Or else, stress in relationships will be your own handiwork and you can't blame others. At the workplace, being too selfish will make you unpopular with your colleagues (trainers) and mess up the atmosphere. Do your work, but do not let your selfishness take total control over you. Be smart about when to do what and when not to.

No badmouthing

Stop talking ill of your colleagues (trainers) to earn a few brownie points with clients. What you think might draw clients to you might actually do the opposite. Instead of talking bad about another trainer's approach or guidance, just talk about YOUR success and the happiness of YOUR clients. And, don't do this every time you see a potential client. Just ensure that the message reaches the person naturally in due course. That will get you more clients as time progresses.

Finding fault

Stop finding fault with your colleagues or you are sure to live in hell. Nobody is perfect, and this includes you too. Let go of certain things because analysing the faults of others will make your mind miserable and, in turn, affect your mind and income too. A person who always finds faults with others will never have friends, will suffer from the lack of a friendly atmosphere at the work spot and will not be successful. Take control of your mind and decide to keep it positive and optimistic. If you talk positive and think positive, you will attract positive vibes.

If you think negative and talk negative, you will attract just that. This is extremely powerful. If you ignore this, nobody can help you.

I spoke about competitors and how to be a successful trainer. Before signing off, there are a few more points I would like to state and these will help you become a successful competitor.

Varinder Ghuman

Be rational in your judgment

We love bodybuilding contests. But many a times we get back from shows with a feeling that we got cheated or our favourite champ was ignored. Is it always true? The answer is an emphatic 'no.'

Stop hero worship

Most of us have favourites. When he loses, we feel bad. Our minds are so much in awe of our favourite that our eyes refuse to scrutinise the line-up of competitors and firmly believes that our man is THE best. This feeling dominates our mind and we are unable to digest a second place even when our favourite genuinely deserves only second.

Peer group

Be it friends or admirers, we are largely influenced by their words. I have seen admirers of champions telling their favourite, 'Bro, you got robbed. You kicked that guy's rear. The judges were partial.'

There have been a few instances when decisions have indeed been wrong. But most of the times, judgments have been decent in most of the shows I have seen. When a champion is surrounded by such people, he will slowly get frustrated and start feeling that the judges will never give him his due. This will eventually ruin the mind and attitude of the competitor who will start feeling, 'they will never give it to me." This will eventually stop the person from giving his 100% to his prep and affect his performance. Needless to say, his performance and placing are sure to go down, affecting him more.

Surround yourself with friends who will always say, 'You will crush your opponent the next time. Let us do it,' and not talk negative. This will help you big time.

Don't misjudge

Don't judge a show by seeing only a couple of photos. Watch all poses and scrutinise all pictures. Watch the videos with an open and unbiased mind. At times, even all these might be a bit deceiving and you might have to watch the show in person to accept the results. A winner should have a great structure, should be symmetrical, proportionally developed, have great shape and excellent condition and decent size. This is how a winner is picked in top shows. Those who lack one or more of these qualities might win in smaller contests but not the bigger ones. A winner should ideally have all these attributes. Learn this well and be fair in your judgment.

Genuine mistakes

If a deserving competitor is genuinely robbed of an award, there is no point in picking a quarrel. Nowhere and at no place has any judge or panel of judges have reversed their judgment. Realise that it is more a point of their ego and nobody will accept that he has done a mistake. Fighting will only bring down your reputation and increase your stress.

Instead, just post your pics and comparison shots on social media without criticising anybody. If you have genuinely been robbed, people will see it. But, you always say that it is ok and that you will not talk ill of anybody. By behaving like a true gentleman, you expose the wrong-doers while simultaneously increasing your image. Just get better for the next show and there will be pressure on the wrong-doers to reward you and not ignore you again. This is the best way out, trust me. Fighting or talking trash is not the way.

There are some more mistakes young athletes commit. Let me shed some light on these topics. Bodybuilding is a fantastic sport. However, if you get your priorities wrong, you are sure to end up extremely frustrated. Avoid the following mistakes if you want to be happy.

Bodybuilding will make me rich

I have seen a lot of young people think like this. This is a very wrong reason to get into bodybuilding in the first place. Please realise that this one of the costliest of sports and you will end up spending tens of thousands of rupees every month on diet and supplements alone, if you are a serious competitor. You need to do this round the year to at least maintain yourself if not to get better. How much money can you actually save? So, a lot of young minds get corrupted by wrong-doers and end up becoming conmen cheating their unsuspecting clients. This is a criminal mistake, which ruins your reputation and affects business in the longer run.

However, if you are smart, you can earn well. For that to happen, you first need to grow to the level of being a celebrity among champions. Then you need to enhance your knowledge, develop your oratory skills and conduct seminars and lectures to earn a decent sum. If you are extremely knowledgeable, you can become a top coach and earn good money. For all this to happen, you need at least a decade and a half of hard, untiring and passionate work. It is not going to happen in a few years, and that is a given. So don't think that you will be the next Jay Cutler or Kris Gethin in a few years and start bodybuilding today. If you are deserving and worthy enough, you can earn.

Job oriented

I still see a lot of youths take up bodybuilding only for getting a job under sports quota. Please do a simple calculation. There are 10 weight categories or so. There are departments like Railways, Services, Postal Department, Ports and Police Department. To get a job under sports quota, an athlete should have won a medal in Senior Mr. India, Junior Mr. India (in a federation recognised by the Union Ministry of Sports) and All-India University National Championship. The age of the person has to be under 24. Now, go and check out the standard in such national events. How many athletes are going to be in this level of competitiveness before 24? Let us assume that even 100 athletes in various weight categories are going to get this good in a given year. Are there going to be vacancies to accommodate all of them this year or may be in a year or two at least? There is no such guarantee. I am not trying to discourage you. All I am saying is don't begin training with the sole aim of getting a job under the sports quota. That, in many cases, will put tremendous stress on young minds and I have seen people getting destroyed when they don't get a job in time.

Instead, love the sport and start training with the sole intention of becoming the best you can be. You might end up with bigger victories than you ever imagined and might get a good job en route. Education is of great importance; so study well. Start doing part-time jobs while making a career as a competitor. Start being a good trainer and make smart moves. You will be extremely successful as time progresses.

Your happiness is YOUR responsibility. Take full control of your life and I guarantee you will be a great champion, a super-successful businessman and a happy family man.

Shruti Kerni

CHAPTER 13

BE A KNOCKOUT – THE POWER OF WOMEN

Even as I was giving finishing touches to *Mind, Muscle, Moksha*, a few of my friends asked me why hadn't I written anything for women. I said all the information I had presented in this book could very well be used by women too. Then, my friends asked me a few specific questions which made me decide that I should perhaps answer them directly so that woman readers who would want to reshape their body get their doubts clarified. So, here goes…

Shweta Rathore

Nishriin Parikh

Ankita Singh

Rita Singh

What are the best techniques to use for a woman to get into shape?

Answer: You can use every single technique presented in *Mind, Muscle, Moksha*. It is not that super sets or DTP or negative reps and so on and so forth are only for men. Depending on a woman's goals, she can use any of these techniques. She can train her muscles once a week or twice a week or once in 3 days or once in 4 or 5 days. The standard 3-day whole body workout and 4-day push-pull split found in the chapter 'Build muscle and lose fat' are perfect even for women.

I am a trainer. What are the main points to focus on when it comes to training a woman?

Answer: If the person is young, has been reasonably active and free from joint and other such nagging issues, she can straight away start with the beginners' programme -- 3 non-consecutive days a week with cardio done on 3 other days. If the person has been inactive and leading a sedentary lifestyle, she first needs a medical check-up. Get her thyroid and other hormone levels, BP, sugar and kidney filtration checked. Also ensure she doesn't have any joint issues. If she does, go by a sports therapist's suggestion. Choose exercises to correct the posture and activate the core. Glute training is extremely important as it strengthens the pelvic floor. Put her on a mild cardio training plan every day for a while even as she is doing her preparatory conditioning work according to the therapist's suggestions. Perfect her diet. She will be ready for a regular workout, most probably, in 2 months unless she has serious injuries or joint issues. When you start, do begin with the beginner's programme. Keep selectorised equipment use to minimum and go more with free weights, tubes and bands. Do not put her into any of the 'bikini body workouts' you might find on the internet. She might not be ready for all that as yet. Be smart.

I am scared to train like what you say in your videos. I don't want to look like my hubby who is trying to compete as a bodybuilder. I see some women showing muscles in their arms…

Answer: A woman can never build hard, dense, ripped muscle like a man mainly because her body produces only a fraction of the male hormone, testosterone. Serious women bodybuilders you see are those who take steroids and that is why they look the way they look. The woman who chooses to stay natural, taking only foods and good quality food supplements, will never look like these women bodybuilders. A natural woman athlete will never get extremely lean and ripped unless she deliberately chooses to cut calories a lot and stay on extended periods of crazy diets, which I don't endorse any way. A woman who is naturally lean might show some separation between her biceps and triceps once she starts working out hard. She still won't gain a lot of size, and that is for sure. If you don't desire even that level of separation, focus on the basics like squats, lunges, hip, glute and calf work with some attention to chest, back and arms. Do a moderate cardio plan twice a week and ensure your diet is rich in essential fats, proteins, lots of fibre and moderate amount of complex carbs. You will not look like a bodybuilder, I promise.

Kavita Nandi

Can I train during my periods?

Answer: A lot of women say they have pain during their periods. Ideally, I would say avoid stressful, heavy exercises like squats, deadlifts, rowing and shoulder press. Choose easier and lighter movements and do fewer sets. Go easy. Go for walking and avoid HIIT kind of work too. Do not exert yourself during this phase. You have 3 ½ weeks in the entire month to train your heart out. Just stick to your diet. Always follow your doctor's suggestion.

Why do you stress so much on fats in your videos?

Answer: Essential Fatty Acids (EFAs) are needed for a plethora of reasons – from repairing cells to helping your body burn stored fat. You need fats for hormonal output too. If you do not consume enough amount of essential fats such Omega 3 and Omega 6 in the perfect ratio, you are just not going to burn all that stored body fat. Your body will conserve every gram of stored fat and won't let go of it. So, ensure you consume enough EFAs, fibre and protein and drink plenty of water.

How do I get rid of cellulite?

Answer: There are no quick fixes. Just get yourself a perfect diet and stay committed to it. Do concentrate on training your thighs, hamstrings and glutes using different exercises. Instead of focussing on weights, focus on getting a great burn in every set. Drink more water than you do now. Topical treatments might have some benefit, or might not have. Just be patient. The results will show. There are fat burning supplements meant for women. If you are a healthy individual, try one from a good company.

Can I ask my client to workout while she is pregnant?

Answer: Here again, go with medical advice. Let the doctor decide when your client is ready for workouts. My wife trained during her second and third trimester. She did light movements and avoided lifts like squats, deadlifts, rows and shoulder press, which increase pressure on the abdominal region. She did a good amount of walking too. She trained even the day before my son was born! Pregnancy training needs medical clearance, careful planning and supervision. Just remember this, there is a feeling in our country that a pregnant woman should eat for two persons. That is not science. Overeating will increase body fat levels and make things difficult – during delivery and post delivery reshaping too. Just ensure that your client eats perfect meals with all nutrients.

Can a woman prevent osteoporosis with workouts?

Answer: Many experts say that a systematic workout done on a regular basis for years, combined with an optimal nutrition plan, can very much help in keeping osteoporosis away. Unless you have a genetic predisposition to

an ailment, a healthy lifestyle can, to a large extent, help you stay healthy and fit for a lifetime. Osteoporosis is basically a loss in bone density. A healthy lifestyle can help prevent it to a significant level; that is what many fitness coaches believe.

Can a lactating woman work out?

Answer: You can. But, there are some experts who say that a very intense programme might actually release some metabolic waste (I am no doctor) in your blood, affecting the quality of milk. I suggest you do a mild workout, just good enough to slowly put you back on track. You can begin a serious comeback plan after some months. Always go with your doctor's suggestion. I am one of those persons who, as a precaution, will tell clients to avoid taking food supplements like creatine or other pharmaceutical grade products while you are in the lactating phase. It might not be the best thing for your baby. Wait for this lactating phase to end. Just eat wholesome foods with enough macros and take the supplements your doctor recommends.

CHAPTER 14

FREQUENTLY ASKED QUESTIONS (FAQS)

M*ind, Muscle, Moksha will be incomplete if I don't answer many of the questions I received. So, apart from those on women, which I presented as a separate chapter, I have put together this section on FAQs as well.*

TRAINING

1. My client is in his 20s. He has reduced 40 kilograms in 11months with only diet and workouts, not using drugs. But, his lower abs and lower chest have developed a "hanging" look. What is the solution?

Mohan Kumar

Siva Kumar

Vinayagam

Sivarama Suthan

Rex Verghese

Sunil Kumar

Sachin Yadav

Pritam Chougule

Abdul Buhari

Answer: Two kilograms a month is the maximum you should lose. Anything faster will make your skin lose elasticity. Remember this -- when your client was too fat, the skin was obviously stretched owing to the fat he was carrying. When he suddenly lost so much fat, the skin was not able to keep pace with it and spread to normal levels. The loose fold of skin that gives a hanging look means that skin has lost elasticity. This can be regained only to a certain extent by regularly massaging with vitamin E oil. Consult a massage therapist and see to what extent it can be set right. If the person is young, the problem can be corrected eventually to a significant extent. If it is worse, consult a cosmetologist or cosmetic surgeon for an expert opinion.

2. Will muscle turn into fat if I stop working out?

Answer: My answer is an emphatic 'No.' When a person stops training, the rate at which his body utilises calories drops down and the body starts to conserve more calories. This leads to fat accumulation. Owing to lack of exercises, lean muscle tissue is broken down, which lowers metabolism further. This, in turn, increases fat accumulation. This creates an illusion as if the muscle has turned into fat. Please understand that muscles can never ever turn into fat. Once a person starts eating right and training hard, the lean muscle can be regained.

3. I can't go to the gym more than twice a week. Tell me how to get a good workout.

Answer: Instead of training only your favourite muscles such as chest and biceps, choose one basic exercise for each major muscle and do 3 sets of 15,12 and 10 reps using the Pyramid principle.

Three sets of squats, bench press, rowing, shoulder press, barbell curls and triceps dips can do a good job. That will be a total of 18 sets. Each set should take about a minute to complete and with just 1 minute rest between sets, your workout will be over in 36 minutes. Ten minutes of warm up and a couple of minutes of cool down (totally 12 minutes) will help you finish the entire session within 50 minutes. Training like this twice a week should still get you decent results, IF your diet is 100% perfect. Apart from this workout, do brisk walking 30 minutes a session twice a week. You need at least two sessions of cardio.

4. Every time I get ready for a contest, I seem to lose muscle. Why is it so?

Answer: If my guess is right, you are drastically cutting carbs as soon as you decide about competing. I would suggest you begin your preparation 5 months before the contest and gradually cut calories. Start cutting about 200 calories from carbs and adding a little protein in the first week of your prep. Week after week, keep cutting carbs and keep adding a small amount of protein. Even as you are doing this, increase cardio sessions, but do not go overboard. This is a general plan and should definitely be tweaked based on the individual's response. Consume enough EFAs and fibre.

In the off-season, stay lean and don't get fat. Your abs should not disappear in the off-season. If it does, you are just lazy.

5. When should I change my workout - once in every 8 weeks or once in 6 weeks?

Answer: I don't think you should change a workout simply because you have done it for 6 weeks or 8 weeks. It is just not necessary. Have a solid diet schedule and start training to gain muscle and lose fat. Keep doing it as long as your plan keeps giving you results. There is no necessity to change a plan that continues to give results. Legends like Arnold Schwarzenegger and Larry Scott have used the same workouts for years, just because the programmes kept giving them results. Some advanced bodybuilders change techniques and exercises every workout or every second or third workout because their bodies need that change to maintain that muscle or grow. This differs from person to person. Until you become a very advanced bodybuilder who can perfectly analyse the feedback from his body and its requirement, do not unnecessarily keep changing things. Please don't change anything because it is boring. Come on, you are not working out to have fun. You are training to get results.

6. My coach tells me to avoid cardio while bulking up. Is it right?

Answer: I'm sorry to say this – this is an archaic practice. Cardio, besides improving heart health, increases appetite, improves nutrient utilization and helps to keep body fat to a minimum in the off-season. Unless you are a super lean, ripped athlete naturally who has very high metabolism and never gains even a little fat despite eating a lot of calories (like Mr. Olympia Dexter Jackson), you should not avoid cardio. I would recommend you do at least 2 sessions of 20 minutes cardio every week even in the off-season if you are a naturally ripped athlete. If you are a normal person, doing 3 sessions of 30 minutes cardio every week in the off-season will be just fine. If you are a person who puts on fat easily, do 20 minutes cardio after your workout 3 to 5 times a week. You just can't avoid this just because you are bulking up. I actually hate the words, 'bulking up.' I prefer using the words 'gaining muscle.' Don't look for excuses to get fat.

7. I am a competitor. Can my wife do the exercises I do? She wants to shape up but does not want to look like me.

Answer: Of course, yes. Tell her not to worry about looking like a man. Read the chapter on women. I am repeating it again. A woman's body does not produce enough testosterone, the male androgenic/anabolic hormone, to build big muscles. Unless you are going to give her anabolic steroids, she is never going to look like a man. Don't give her even milder drugs like Anavar or strong fat loss drugs like Clen. Just put her on a good diet and fat burners meant specifically for women (if she doesn't mind taking them). Be very clear that a woman who trains with weight will have shapely, tight, lean muscle, which will increase metabolism. This will help her to burn more fat even while resting. Squats, lunges, barbell hip thrusts, deadlifts, push ups, dumbbell rows, dumbbell chest presses, dumbbell curls and triceps extensions are some of the exercises she should do. She can do plyometrics eventually and cardio should also be performed adequate number of times based on the individual's necessity. Science says that a woman can gain about 80% the strength of a man while gaining less than one tenth of his size.

8. Tell me how to find out whether a person is taking drugs.

Answer: It is just by years of watching how various physiques look and change that we learn a lot. Experience can tell us whether the person we are looking at might or might not have taken drugs. I have some general points to offer though. A person who is on the 'gear' will have a physique that looks hard, a kind of look that makes us wonder if he has been carved out of a rock. Only a very few people who train naturally have this kind of look. The second thing that should catch our eye is that the person's skin – it would be paper-thin and the muscle fibres might look awesome. A couple of sets of pumping might dramatically change the appearance of those muscles and make them come alive, looking as if they are going to tear away the skin and burst out. The third aspect is the vascularity -- the veins might look big and thick. Though veins show well if a person's body fat percentage is low, a drug user will have increase blood volume, which might give him awesome pumps, thereby making the veins look like garden hoses! Apart from all these, the cosmetic side effects such as gynaecomastia on a hard, muscular physique are always going to be clear signs of drug use.

9. Do I need a personal trainer or coach?

Answer: A coach, who is well informed, takes the guesswork out of your game plan. He does all the planning on diet and workout, which you just follow and get results. Ideally, he should be the one who is on the gym floor pushing you hard. Even if that is not happening, a good coach is of great value.

As regards a personal trainer, he should be able to assess when you are really tired and when you should not be pushed hard. A trainer is not a repetition counting robot. He should

keep you energetic, optimistic and charged up all through the session. If you are able to do it on your own and do the exercises with optimal intensity, you might not need a personal trainer. It is up to the individual. A good trainer, too, brings a lot of value, let me add. General trainers cannot stand by the side of just one client and that makes it necessary for a person to hire a personal trainer. In many cases, good trainers matter more than a super-equipped gym. A place can be awesome, but if the trainers are those who merely rely on performance enhancing drugs to do their transformation, the place is as good as non-existent. Even with very basic equipment, accessories and treadmills, a place with knowledgeable trainers (who just don't put every single client on drugs) is a hundred times better than a posh and furnished glossy gym.

10. Do you recommend the use of knee wraps, wrist straps and weight belts?

Answer: I do when it is necessary. Use of weight belts is a must when you use extreme poundage and not suboptimal weights. Using belts always might prevent the smaller stabiliser muscles from getting strong, according to experts. Use knee wraps only on the heaviest set of squats, deadlifts and leg presses. I personally never liked lifting straps because I did not feel comfortable. However, most trainers swear by their effectiveness. Try them out.

11. Can a good trainee eventually become a good trainer?

Answer: He might, provided he is smart and learns well.

12. Will masturbation and sex affect muscle growth?

Answer: If you masturbate too frequently, you might run out of gas. It might have a negative impact on certain other aspects in your life. But will it affect muscle growth? Not directly, at least. If you don't recover owing to crazy practices, your training might actually put you on track to losing muscle. In that way, it might have an effect. Never do anything that might affect recovery. As regards sex, it will have least negative effects, unless you are so dumb to do all circus for a few hours, just jump out of the bed and head straight to the gym to battle big weights for a few hours.

NUTRITION

I am a competitor. What can I do to stay committed to my diet. I am finding it very hard to diet and avoid eating tasty food.

Answer: It is immaterial if you are a competitor or not. Just try out this trick – take copies of a picture of yours, either in your best shape or in your current shape. Put it on your mobile phone as screen saver, on your fridge door, almirah doors, and every single place which you are going to see throughout the day. If you keep on seeing how good you used to look or how pathetic you look right now, you will not be tempted to eat cheat foods. This trick has helped a lot of people. Try it, it works big time.

Will a high-protein diet affect my health?

Answer: According to the general recommendation, a sedentary person might need about 0.8 gm of protein for every kilogram of body weight. A person who starts serious weight training needs at least 2 to 2.2 gm of protein for every kilogram of lean body weight to build lean muscle. This might be high protein for a sedentary person, but the adequate level for a serious bodybuilder. A healthy person who gets into bodybuilding will not be affected by consuming this amount of protein. Eating too less will force the person's body to break down lean muscle, slow down metabolism and affect immunity too. Just ensure that you drink plenty of water (we recommend around 5 to 6 litres a day depending upon the individual). Add enough alkaline foods to your diet without fail. Take enough EFAs and a fibre supplement.

Tell me the best meal I can eat before a workout.

Answer: A pre-workout meal is as important as a post-workout meal. Researchers say that those who drink a protein shake 20 minutes before a weight training session increase their metabolic rate by 8% when compared to those who consume only a carbohydrate drink. In general, eating a solid meal 45 to 60 minutes before a workout is a very good plan. Eat some egg whites and sweet potato in that meal. This will give enough carbohydrates to fuel an intense workout and amino acids to preserve muscle tissue. Finish the workout within an hour max and immediately drink a fast-acting protein like whey. Eat another solid meal within 30 minutes.

I just want to tone my body. So I don't think much protein is needed.

Answer: Please be clear that there is no such thing like "toning." This is a term often used to signify the addition of a small amount of lean muscle while reducing fat. But to gain even that little amount of lean muscle, a person training hard at the gym should consume 2 gm of protein for every kilogram of his or her bodyweight. If your protein intake is lower, especially when you cut calories to lose fat, the body will cannibalise (break down) lean muscle. This is called catabolism, which slows the calorific expenditure rate. To add a small amount of muscle to get that toned look, eat the correct amount of calories needed and the right amount of protein. Don't do any guess work. Get a weight training and cardio programme that suits your goals and don't train like a bodybuilder who would want to gain more and more size. My suggestion is that you use free weights, learn about functional training, and do a couple of sessions of cardio with this.

What has satiety got to do with fat loss?

Answer: Simple. You will avoid unnecessary snacking. This will help in two ways – it will help in regulating insulin output and prevent in consumption of unwanted calories. As I always insist, take enough protein with essential fats and fibre. Consume the amount of complex carbs you need. You will be on the right track.

Acknowledgements

There are a lot of people who have encouraged me to write this book. There are some who have helped me to make *Mind, Muscle, Moksha* one of the best physique training guides possible.

I sincerely thank all of them as this book would not have been possible without their encouragement and support.

My special thanks to T.A. Narasimhan, Managing Editor, *The Hindu*; N. Venkateshwaran, News Editor, *The Hindu*; Vasanth Srinivasan, Senior Editor, *BusinessLine*; and Kannan Sundar, Deputy National Design Editor, *The Hindu*, who have supported me right from the day I decided to write this book.

I thank my mentor Olympia Jai, all the master coaches and champions who have been sharing information with me.

I am indebted to all the people who have been following my articles and information which I have been sharing free of cost over the past two decades. Your love and support have helped me come a long way from humble beginnings.

I dedicate *Mind, Muscle, Moksha* to all of you who have made me what I am today.

BEFORE SIGNING OFF...

Mind, Muscle, Moksha was written with a clear objective of providing the best information to any person, man or woman, who wishes to sculpt his/her body. *Mind, Muscle, Moksha*, I am sure, has touched upon most of the training techniques, tricks and practices in vogue among physique coaches and champions.

I once again repeat that I don't endorse all practices, especially the extreme ones, that are being tried out. This book would be, according to me, incomplete if I refused to even mention what is happening in the sport and that was the intention behind writing about those practices too.

Mind, Muscle, Moksha, I am confident, will be the most reliable training partner you can have in achieving your physique goals.

Stop wasting another workout; stop getting exploited by those who tell you that they know the tricks to getting a great body; stop wasting money on worthless supplements and start focussing on a solid nutrition and training programme.

Your results will speak louder than your words on social media.

Good luck.